Riding the Samoosa Express

First published by Modjaji Books (Pty) Ltd 2014
PO Box 385, Athlone, 7760, Cape Town, South Africa
www.modjajibooks.co.za

ISBN 978-1-920590-32-1
e-book ISBN 978-1-920590-94-9

Book and cover design by Megan Ross
Cover artwork by Carla Kreuser

Printed and bound by Megadigital, Cape Town
Set in Garamond

Riding the Samoosa Express

PERSONAL NARRATIVES OF MARRIAGE AND BEYOND

EDITED BY ZAHEERA JINA AND HASINA ASVAT

modjaji books

Dedicated with love to all the Muslim women who shared their stories.

PART ONE

The road towards marriage

PART TWO

Identity

PART THREE

Marriage and beyond

INTRODUCTION

It all started with a simple conversation about the exchange of photographs. My cousin, Shameema, was single and the prospective "Mr Right" had asked to see a photograph of her before taking the quest further. When I asked her for a photograph to send to him she refused, saying that she would first like to see his photograph and curriculum vitae and that she would make the final decision about whether to meet him. Her response did not fit in with my frame of reference. I did not agree with the practice of sending around photographs, but, to me, the road to meeting "Mr Right" was still about the traditional idea of men making the first request, not the other way around. I believe in the notion of the "samoosa run", or "samoosa express to marriage", which are the terms used to describe the meeting when eligible Muslim men go alone or with family members to see prospective wives at their homes. Shameema is a chartered accountant and partner at the firm where she works. At thirty she is content in her own shell and definitely does not need marriage to make her feel complete. Our short conversation got me thinking about social and religious expectations and, of course, about the identity of the professional Muslim woman.

I was single for many years and during this time had many visits from different "Mr Eligibles" and their families. I also became a teacher and worked for a while. I then embarked on postgraduate studies and chose a career in academia. Most weekends were spent in entertaining the prospective husbands-to-be who came from far and wide but, to them, I was always "too educated" or "too tall". Eventually, I met my husband through an arrangement between my niece and my sister-in-law.

Being single did not make my life feel complete. I yearned to be a wife, housewife and mother. I was willing to give up working towards a PhD for the gift of marriage. I saw the goal of obtaining a PhD as an occupation that could fill my lonely days as a single woman. I was brought up in a home where my mother gave up her profession in nursing to look after me and my siblings when we were young children. She then studied towards teaching, and worked as a preschool teacher when we were at school. For my mother, at the time, giving up her nursing profession was expected of her as a Muslim mother and wife. My father certainly expected nothing less. As a woman from a later generation, I have been entrusted with the choice to complete my studies after marrying and while raising a family. However, in making the choice, I am often plagued with uncertainty about who I truly am – a modern, PhD Mum; or a traditional, homely wife. While pondering on my own, personal identity, I considered the lives of others and, after discussing the idea with a friend, I decided to compile an anthology of narratives written by professional or well-educated Muslim women

I had anecdotal evidence about the difficulty of being a professional Muslim woman as South Africa's history changed. I had witnessed how friends and family members struggled to maintain professions and juggle family life, but I wanted to know more about their life journeys. My experience reminded me that Islam as a religious system did not encourage women to study or to pursue their professions. Many Muslim men, even today, do not want professional or career-driven wives. Under the laws of apartheid, in the 1960s and 1970s Indians were only allowed entrance to teaching or nursing. Muslim parents during those decades adhered to the belief that their female children should learn only how to perform skills like cooking and sewing. The conditions and trends have changed since then, with many Muslim women fulfilling their dreams in every profession possible.

The global ideology that prevails around the subject of Muslim women has been shaped by a description of them as voiceless, silent and oppressed. Other views have positioned Muslim women as either religious or secular and have ignored the complexity of their experiences (Davids, 2003). In South Africa, however, Muslim women have been able to participate in secular education and employment opportunities and to practise their religion within the privilege of a democracy that is open to issues of gender. In 2008, Sader concluded a study called *The Identity of Muslim Women in South Africa: Married Couples' Perspectives* which provides insight into the identity construction of South African Muslim women of Indian descent who are married, educated and working in post-apartheid South Africa. Sader showed that these women prioritised an Islamic identity and were able to construct an alternative identity which allowed them the freedom to access secular spaces, or what may be viewed as the public sphere of men. Other South African research concerning Muslim women includes aims to develop an understanding of attitudes, beliefs and practices of Muslim women within South African communities in relation to marriage, sexuality and gender (Shaikh, 1996; Shaikh, 2002).

This book is not a research project and it does not make any points or arguments in relation to Muslim women. It is a collection of life-stories. I wanted to find out about the achievements and accomplishments Muslim women have managed. I needed to know how others were juggling their lives and daily routines to make their dreams a reality. The call for stories encouraged contributors to explore issues of love, loss, family life, culture, religious beliefs, suburban life, local and international politics, freedom, and education, among other important issues. I wanted the contributors to find themselves in their stories; I wanted them to write honest descriptions of who they are as Muslim women, their journeys to self-discovery or their questions about their identities. I believe that there's a stark essence in every woman's own story, written from her soul. I received an overwhelming response to the call for submissions, and I was both awed and humbled by the many stories received.

The collection begins with the story that sets the scene around the concept of marriage in the context of religion and culture, Farhana Ismail's "Education and *Izzat!*" and from there – together with Hasina Asvat, my sister-in-law and partner in editing – I tried to compile a selection of stories that best represents a full range of experiences. The submissions that I received reflect a central focus of marriage. Marriage defines the status of a Muslim woman through societal expectations and religious beliefs. Marriage forms the apex of the lives of many Muslim women because of their Islamic obligation to it. It is believed by Muslims that Prophet Muhammad (SAW) said, "When a man marries, he has fulfilled half of his religion, so let him fear Allah regarding the remaining half." The stories that make up this compilation give breath to these philosophies through thoughts and understandings from women who are in agreement and those who question.

Muslim women need to be heard and our stories need to be told. This book aims to be a testimony of our journey.

I've arranged the stories in this book into three parts. Part One, "The road towards marriage", includes stories of finding (or not) a marriage partner in the light of religious beliefs and cultural and societal expectations. Part Two, "Identity", tells stories of women trying to find themselves, in religion, or as working women, or in the home. And Part Three, "Marriage and beyond", features stories from contributors of their lives when married and in trying to deal with the ups and downs of life. Stories include the experiences of childbearing, the grieving of the passing of loved ones and struggles with depression.

Being a Muslim woman involves a perfect blend of spices, philosophies and rituals. Only through descriptions of their lives are we allowed to walk with some of these women, see what they see, and try to understand the complexity of a Muslim woman's life.

Zaheera Jina

References

Davids, L. (2003). *Positioning Muslim Women: A Feminist Narrative Analysis.* Annual Review of Islam in South Africa.

Sader, F. (2008). *The Identity of Muslim Women in South Africa: Married Couples' Perspectives.* Master's Thesis, University of the Witwatersrand.

Shaikh, S. (1996). *Battered Women in Muslim Communities: Religious Constructions of Gender, Marriage, Sexuality and Violence:* Master's Thesis, University of Cape Town.

Shaikh, S. (2002). *Transforming Feminisms: Islam, Women and Gender Justice.* Seminar paper, Department of Religious Studies, University of Cape Town.

PART ONE

The road towards marriage

Education and *Izzat*!

Farhana Ismail

"You are taking my *izzat* away!" yelled my father, again. If my dad had ever allowed his hair to grow, having me as a daughter would have caused him to lose it many years ago. I could just imagine him pulling it out every time we had one of our epic spats.

I grew up with very traditional[i] parents in very unusual circumstances for that time. My three younger brothers and I were told that education was extremely important. We had to work hard at school. Faizel, the elder of my three brothers, and I would earn extra pocket money working as sales people in a clothing store in Johannesburg. Education, resourcefulness, and self-reliance were emphasised. I don't think any of us realised what that education actually entailed – least of all my parents.

My parents had sent us to a private school to avoid the system of apartheid education. They believed they were giving us many more opportunities than we would have had if we had stayed in the government education system and gone to Indian schools. Everyone knew that white kids had the best schools and facilities, and private schools provided both. Every last cent was put into education. Mum and Dad worked late nights and long hours to pay school fees.

It was the eighties and South Africa was on the cusp of political upheaval. At school we were encouraged to question authority, challenge it, and push the boundaries of conservatism, tradition, nd prejudice in all its forms – including gender discrimination – in our journey towards creating a new ideal society. For me, an Indian Muslim girl growing up in Johannesburg, that also meant questioning the traditional role of South African Muslim women in the home and in society – particularly our exclusion from the sacred space of the mosque.

It was in this arena of cultural-religious practice that my dad and I clashed. "Why do you insist on sitting in the room when the *jamaat* come? Asking questions about women in mosques. Just leave them alone! You are taking my *izzat* away!" he would lament.

That our school had an impressive record of churning out doctors, lawyers, accountants, engineers and, as in my case, optometrists, was a bonus. Mum and Dad, though, weren't prepared for the activism that lurked beneath the surface: our school at the time was also a breeding ground for activists.

And so, when I questioned the gender bias in my religion and in my cultural practices, or worse, when I chose to travel to an Arab land (of all places on earth) to pursue studies in Arabic with a group of twenty other young women, my dad's blood pressure sky-rocketed.

"Listen to me! You will get kidnapped by Arab slave owners and sold." His arguments were purely emotional; they were not based on any precept in Islamic law or on current events.

It was against this backdrop that my own journey into marriage and beyond began.

Expectations and suitors

Without saying a thing, my parents had managed to convey the message that I was expected to, at some point, get married. My mother, like any good, loving Indian mother, made numerous unsuccessful attempts at teaching me the rudimentary steps of Indian cooking. She is a very good cook, as was her mother, my *Nanima*, and so my lack of effort and interest in this totally baffled her.

"*Rotis* are not meant to be square!" Slap! The flat-end of the spatula would hit the back of my hand. She and I would have endless fights over why only I and not my brothers had to spend precious free time in the kitchen.

"How much salt, Mummy?" I would ask.

"*Ahre*," she would answer, much to my disgust. I wanted precise measurements.

My dad would often tell me to dress in a more lady-like manner and to look neat. Growing up with three brothers, and a naturally beautiful mother who was relatively uninterested in fashion, my dress sense had not become refined. And the grunge look didn't appeal to my dad.

While my parents carefully didn't mention that I should marry, for fear of reprisals like, "Oh! So you want to get rid of me!", well-meaning, troublesome aunties had no such scruples. It also didn't help that I was the oldest girl grandchild on my mum's side. These wonderful, entertaining aunties and grandaunts had no one else to pester!

They would tell me when I had turned twenty-one, "You're not getting any younger, you know."

"You have to stop being so choosy."

"Don't let your chances slip by."

This last comment was made after I refused a marriage proposal from a good-looking, BMW-owner from KwaZulu-Natal. His main attraction for the elders in my family, however, wasn't his BMW or his charming smile. What mattered most was that he was a *Khanamia* boy. In other words, his great-grandparents came from the same village in Gujerat, India, which my great-grandparents hailed from, too. That made them practically family, and therefore good marriage material. If they were *Khanamia*, then they were more acceptable. And so we had some hopeful young men visiting us, in search of a good *Khanamia* Muslim girl. In this mix were a couple of doctors, a drug addict and a future wife beater (this was only revealed a year later, during his marriage to someone else). And so it went on, one suitor after another.

I, of course, attributed my persistent stubbornness as the reason for my lucky escape from these undesirable matches. I likened these arranged viewing visits to a cattle show. And I refused to dress up or carry in the tea – as was the Indian tradition.

My three younger brothers, in the meantime, remained under the radar, while I, the girl, dealt with everyone's marriage expectations. My brothers would mostly observe and enjoy the spectacle being played out. And sometimes they would participate – much to the embarrassment of my mum and grandma and the disgust of my dad.

Once, a bearded young man came visiting with his mum. We would always try to get a glimpse of the hopeful suitor as he entered the front door. The covered balcony of my bedroom was adjacent to the front door. There was a door leading out onto the common porch area. And so we would all belly-crawl onto the balcony, so that we could observe without being seen. On this occasion, after getting a glimpse of the mature-looking man, my brothers decided to have some fun.

All three brothers joined me as I reluctantly went to greet the visitors. My middle brother, Azhar, sat directly opposite my suitor and proceeded to stare him down, for the duration of the visit. Muhammad, who was about six years old at the time, rolled a ball back and forth in front of the poor man. But it was my eldest brother, Faizel, whose antics mortified my parents and *Nanima.*

Dressed in his standard torn track pants, he faced the room, leaning nonchalantly against the mantle-piece. Crossing his not-too-clean bare feet, he picked up the latest copy of the progressive community newspaper, *al-Qalam*, waved it about in front of the hopeful suitor, and said mischievously, "So! Have you seen the article about women insisting on going to the mosques? What's your take on the issue?"

Villages and a wedding date

The first time Ashraff, my husband, came home to meet my parents, Dad asked him, "So … which *gaam* are you from?"

Ashraff, who knew too well what the answer should be, said, "um … Wakkerstroom, South Africa?"

"Yes. But in India. Which *gaam* in India?"

"I don't know! But I'm sure it's from the wrong side of the river," was his cheeky reply.

Ashraff and I met through Faizel, in the early nineties. I had already graduated, and was working. Faizel and I had had many theological disagreements and he finally invited me to join his *halqah* on campus. At the time, he was studying law at Wits.

Being part of the *halqah* was a transformative process for me. Through it, I was exposed to contemporary Islamic literature on a wide range of subjects – law, economics, politics, and gender. I was introduced to the ideology of the progressive international Islamic movement, and met members of the local Muslim Youth Movement (MYM). We read the works of many classical and religious scholars. Through vigorous debates and discussions, the *halqah* began to shape my understanding of Islam and helped me to discover my unique Muslim identity.

And then in 1994, at the age of twenty-two, I applied to join a group of girls to study Arabic in Jordan. My dad was totally against the idea. But Mum and *Nanima* were quite supportive, so I went ahead.

It was during my year away that Ashraff and I got to know one another better.

Our correspondence, mainly through phone calls and letters was a cause of great jubilation and excitement for my roommates in Jordan. They enjoyed teasing us.

On my return from an enriching Middle Eastern adventure in 1995, I was firmer in my female Muslim identity. I had always experienced a disconnection between the pragmatic system of Islam and its ethical vision. And, over time, I had become better informed. Through my readings and research, I had begun to experience in the primary texts, the Quran and the examples of the Prophets, a religion that testifies to the absolute moral and spiritual equality of men and women. I had studied verses in the Quran that speak to both men and women as active participants in building a just society. In these verses believers are referred to as men and women, who are friends and protectors to one another, enjoining what is good and forbidding what is not. (For example, see *Surah* Taubah, verse 71.)

Ashraff too, had been questioning his patriarchal experiences of Islam and he had embarked on his own journey through the progressive writings of Muslim intellectuals and the *halqah*.

A month after my return, we decided to marry. My parents definitely did not condone dating, and because I refused to lie to them, a protracted courtship outside of marriage was out of the question.

I had observed the Arab way of marriage where a *nikah* is first contracted, and the courtship happens thereafter. If the couple decides that it will not work out, the *nikah* will simply be annulled. If they like each other, the wedding reception will go ahead a few months later, and the bride and groom will then live together. This really appealed to me, because it would give me an opportunity to get to know Ashraff better without having to lie or feel guilty. But both our families rejected the idea. "That's just not how it's done in South Africa."

In South Africa the *nikah* is contracted, followed by the wedding reception (usually within a few hours after the *nikah*) and the couple live together thereafter with a divorce being the only annulment. A courtship prior to marriage (although common) is considered sinful. And so instead, we set the earliest wedding date we could possibly find, much to my dad's dismay. "Listen to me! Why rush it? Wait a bit. You may just change your mind. You never know," he pleaded.

"Be honest! It's because he isn't *Khanamia*. It's because he's *Surtee*, isn't it? That's why you're being so discouraging," I retorted.

"Don't be stupid. What do we know of him or his family?" pleaded my dad.

Faizel, of course, was no help. He just managed to further antagonise our dad.

We finally set the date for what later turned out to be the coldest night of 1996.

But the heat had turned up so much in the pre-wedding build up, that some of us hadn't even noticed the weather!

A mosque and a hall

The only affordable venue available at the time turned out to be the Marlboro Hall adjacent to the Marlboro mosque, north of Johannesburg. It was after we booked the venue that the controversy began.

Ashraff and I had decided that we would both have to be present at our *nikah* and that I would actively participate and give my direct consent to the marriage. Although this was a practice in other parts of the Muslim world and it wasn't contrary to Islamic law, it was certainly flouting South African Muslim tradition.

In South Africa, the bride gives her consent to her *wali* and signs the marriage register, either the day before or a few hours before the *nikah*. Her *wali* acts as her representative during the marriage ceremony, which is presided over by the *Imam*, and at which all the male members of the marriage party are present. The ceremony is usually held in the mosque, in the absence of the bride and all other women. Most mosques in Johannesburg at the time did not allow women inside. And Marlboro mosque was one of these. This practice was, of course, contrary to Islamic teachings. The primary sources of Islamic law definitely do not exclude women from sacred spaces such as mosques.

What this meant for us in 1996, though, was that, as much as we wanted to, we couldn't perform the *nikah* ceremony in the Marlboro mosque and had to do it in the adjacent hall instead. This was very difficult for a number of members of my extended family to understand. They were a lot more traditional in their Islamic practice and it seemed to them like we were tempting fate by not having the ceremony in the holy sanctity of the mosque. Ashraff's family didn't say much, except that they were just happy he was getting married!

After some discussion, though, my dad reluctantly agreed to have the ceremony in the hall.

"I have one condition," he said. "The person doing the *nikah* has to be a recognised *Imam* – with a beard!"

And it was here that we found the most resistance.

The Imams and the Sheikh

In Islam, marriage is highly recommended. Men and women are encouraged to marry. In fact, according to an often-quoted saying of the Prophet Muhammad (*SAW*), "Whoever has married has completed half of his religion; therefore let him fear Allah in the other half!" (Al Bayhaqi.) The *Quran* mentions the love and compassion found in marriage as one of the signs of God's existence: "And among His signs is this: that He created for you spouses from among yourselves, so that you might find rest in them; and has set between you love and compassion. Truly there are signs in this for people who reflect." (*Surah* Rum, verse 21.)

And so, if marriage is such an important step that Allah mentions it as a sign of his existence, and the Prophet spoke of it as being "half the religion," we were confident that even the most conservative of *Imams* would see it as his Islamic duty to assist us.

But we were mistaken.

The *Imam* of Marlboro mosque initially agreed, but on hearing of our plans to have the *nikah* in the hall, flatly refused. It turned out that every other *Imam* Ashraff approached had the same objection. No one would agree to contravene protocol and do the *nikah* in the hall, especially because the mosque was right next door.

In a telephone conversation with one *Imam*, Ashraff explained that if I were allowed access to the mosque we would gladly have the *nikah* there. The *Imam* on the other end of the line rejoined, "Tell your future wife to get her priorities straight!"

And so I took his advice, and instead of focusing on the décor, the flowers or even the music, I proceeded to help find an *Imam*. On the last night before the wedding, we still hadn't found someone to conduct the ceremony. It was then that we began to panic.

Shamima Shaikh, a MYM friend, suggested we ask her father, Sheikh Salahuddin, a *madressah* teacher from Pietersburg, a city three hours away from Johannesburg. With his long, graying beard, humorous twinkle in his eye, and tranquil, dignified manner, Sheikh Salahuddin turned out to be the perfect person for our unconventional ceremony. His calm influence was definitely needed, especially because Ashraff and I had broken with tradition in other ways too. We had decided to negotiate a personalised Islamic marriage contract and our master of ceremonies, Naeem Jeenah, (Sheikh Salahuddin's son-in-law) had decided to read out parts of our contract at our wedding. To say that mouths dropped would be an understatement!

The sacred and the unholy

In Islam, marriage is essentially a contract between two consenting parties. It is, however, distinguished from an ordinary contract in that it is sacred and has love as the necessary component. Islamic history points to numerous examples of men and women who negotiated the terms of their marriage contract to suit their own specific circumstances. Prophet Muhammad's (*SAW*) great granddaughter, Sukayna, was known for her interesting negotiations in this regard.

She had married numerous times, and in one instance had stated in her marriage contract that she should live near one of her closest friends. Scholars such as al-Tabari encouraged contracts and went as far as to make provision for women to limit polygamy in their contracts.

Negotiations around such a marriage contract would be a form of pre-marital counselling and would set the stage for a better understanding and management of each others' expectations. In this way the contract would protect and maintain the spirit of openness, trust, mutual respect, loyalty and co-operation in the marriage. Ashraff and I were well aware of the benefits of such a contract and, when Shamima and Naeem offered to assist us, we agreed to draw one up together.

Over a period of two weeks we discussed the terms of our contract. This included practical aspects like the dowry amount, the matrimonial property regime, financial rights and obligations, as well as social and family obligations[ii]. We wrangled over thornier issues, like dispute-resolution procedures and divorce matters – the different types of divorce, and the Islamic law on maintenance and custody.

Most of our friends and family had never heard or seen a marriage contract of this nature, and when Naeem first mentioned it in his speech as master of ceremonies at our wedding, they were mildly surprised. It was only after he read out some excerpts though, that they were stunned. Even I cringed.

"Farhana's and Ashraff's contract deals with the distribution of household responsibilities and even governs sexual relations in their marriage," he told everyone gathered there. "For example, it states that sexual relations will be based on mutual respect and trust and that such relations depend on the mutual agreement of them both."

With that one statement, the background murmur that normally accompanies a wedding speech completely disappeared. For a brief moment every person there was asking himself or herself, "Did I hear correctly? Did he just say that?!"

Some family members later reported that they had choked on the savouries they had been sampling. One of my uncles, instead of congratulating Ashraff after the *nikah*, said disparagingly, "Your contract is a whole lot of hogwash!" Some of Ashraff's cousins chortled that they hadn't had so much fun at a wedding in a long time. And *Nanima* apparently put her head in her hands and said in her vernacular Gujerati, "*Aieee! Ai poiri hu kare*?!"

Crossing floors and waiting tables

Amidst all the drama of finding the *Imam* and negotiating a contract, I had just managed to organise, with the help of close friend Naseema Mustapha, a fun belly-dancing *mendhi* evening for my cousins and girlfriends. I had a modest wedding dress, but no clue as to other details of the wedding, like the menu and décor.

My loving aunties, in spite of all their reservations about my stubborn stipulations, stepped in. They organised the flowers and managed to make the hall look festive enough. It was only when some of my uncles got involved that I was mildly bothered. Ashraff and I had planned to contract our *nikah* at a table at the front of the hall. We wanted to be at the same table, with the *Imam* and witnesses accompanying us. But some uncles would not hear of this. Without telling us, they arranged two separate tables at opposite ends of the hall, one for the bride and one for the groom's party and the *Imam*.

What this meant was that my *wali* and two witnesses walked to my table and asked me if I would marry Ashraff. After I said, "yes", they proceeded to amble in a solemn convoy all the way down the length of the hall, past the 600 guests, to the table at the back, where the marriage ceremony then commenced. After the final *duah*, Ashraff then walked the length of the hall to my table. The whole process was so absurd that I felt like shrieking with suppressed laughter. Luckily, I managed to contain myself.

Ours was one of the last of those Indian weddings in which everyone your dad and mum knows are invited, where the budget goes into feeding 600 people, and where there are no caterers or expensive decorations.

And so, all the men and boys in my family had to roll up their sleeves and work.

They acted as waiters, served the food, and helped to clean up after. Even my brother's Christian friend, Dario, who had come in his best suit, hung up his jacket, rolled up his sleeves and pitched in. And apart from an uncle getting locked in the toilet, there were no more glitches that evening – that is, until we returned home.

Dangling legs and (un)customary send offs

When Ashraff and I, accompanied by our best friends, Zakiyya and Ahmed, drove up to the front gate of my parents' house, we were met with a wacky scene.

Most of the members of my wedding party were standing outside in the freezing cold trying to keep warm. A stepladder was propped up against the side of the house, and my dad's legs were dangling out of a narrow balcony window. He had misplaced the house keys and had apparently found a way to let us into the house.

In the meantime, Ashraff's family had decided to break with tradition. Instead of coming home to "fetch" me, they had started the journey back to Wakkerstroom, a good three hours away. The road was not well lit and was treacherous at night, and they were anxious to get back because they were hosting the *walimah* the next day. En route, his cousin, who was driving, hit a cow, but luckily emerged unhurt.

But even this didn't match the drama that was unfolding at my parents' house.

We were all sitting around, sipping cups of hot, masala tea, when my dad realised that something was amiss – I was still there – happily enjoying the delicious brewed tea. This could only mean one thing: once again, this tedious daughter, and now his son-in-law too, had broken with precious tradition.

He was not happy. "What nonsense! It's tradition! They must come to my house to fetch my daughter! It's about my *izzat*!" he fumed.

Ashraff's family apologised to him the next day, but it took many years before dad's *izzat* was sufficiently restored.

And then my brother Faizel got married!

Exiting limbo

Anonymous

Here I was, at this metaphorical "station" called nowhere. I came to be here by a series of events, or non-events if you will. I come from a conservative, middle class, Islamic family. Like most of the girls in our family, I have had very little formal education. Leaving school at a young age, we were sent away to further our Islamic studies. It was somewhat difficult, being that I was young and far from home, but nonetheless, a most enlightening time. Soon, it was over, and I returned home and set out helping in the family business. Before I knew it, I was being educated in the art of cooking and baking. Marriage would follow soon after, I was told. This is one of those very odd times in one's life. The reason being that you're told at a young age to shy away from the opposite sex, and then the next thing you know, you're sitting "ALONE" with a total stranger and everyone's okay with it! Even more weird is that you're expected to learn enough about this person in the ensuing fifteen minutes to be able to decide the rest of your future! Totally scary! This went on for some time, with no luck.

And then fate stepped in … I had developed a serious case of atopic dermatitis, or eczema. Hardly life threatening, but nevertheless, my real trial had begun. Initial treatments with pharmaceuticals worked wonders. Oh joy! That was until the recurrence of the illness. Eventually I could no longer use these medications as the side effects had taken a toll on my body. I then opted for a homeopathic trial. It's funny how they tell you that your condition is most likely to worsen before it improves. They, however, fail to mention as to just how much worse it would get. And so it did … there was a point where I could barely walk. Being a good patient, I continued with the treatments.

However, six months later, I called it quits. I wasn't allowed most foods, and with this strict dieting, and medication, I had not improved. What followed were many cases of trial and error. During this time I had continued to be "showcased". My eczema dominated my hands, and as a result I used them very little. Pustules covered every inch of my hands resulting in insane itching, cuts, bleeding and almost paralytic pain. Virtually everything I came into contact with caused a flare up. I was unable to cook or clean without suffering, so I gave it up altogether. Of course, this did not help with possible suitors. Our background, culture and society believe that the woman is the heart of the home. I clearly did not fit this picture.

After much deliberation, I came to a decision to remove myself to the proverbial shelf. This was met with great disdain and disappointment. No one really understood, even though I had explained over and over why I had come to this decision. It made no sense to me to burden another with my illness. How could I do that? It just wasn't in me. People I had known almost all my life ridiculed me, and belittled my sickness, accusing me of exaggerating it. I was told that there were people worse off than me, who lived full lives, who "did" things despite their troubles. I was dubbed a lazy, good for nothing, who was a burden on her family. I was the girl mothers warned their daughters never to be like. This was a most difficult time. I was hurt and embarrassed, my self-esteem and confidence all but depleted, and I was borderline depressive. I hated being this weak person. It was very frustrating. I was fortunate, however, to have the help and support of friends and family, and I managed to regain some semblance of self-respect. Doctor after doctor tried their best, with each treatment working in the initial stages; however, there was no long term success. My eczema, with a life of its own, would come back angrier, and meaner, as if seeking revenge for being banished.

As the years passed, and my parents grew older, they were plagued with concern about who would care for me in the event that they were to meet their *Creator*. As I had very little formal education, I was unable to study or work. And the skills I did have were without any use. But as time lapsed, doors began to open. I was now older and therefore no longer required a higher education to get one!

Ten years, and some twenty odd doctors later, I have come to know myself and my illness a little better. I've subsequently learnt what triggers flare ups, and how to avoid these. Unfortunately there are those that elude me, only to manifest on my skin sooner or later. I've been told that there is no cure, that I will need continuous medication for the rest of my life. I'd like to not lose hope and believe otherwise.

I am twenty eight now and an aspiring writer. I am also studying child psychology. I hope to start a school of higher education for girls some day. I'd like to help them understand that they are capable of contributing so much more than society allows them to believe … My illness has made me a stronger, greatly empathic, and better person. They say that things happen for a reason, and that Allah works in mysterious ways, perhaps this is testament to that. Yes, I do have bad days, but with my loved ones around me, it lightens the load. I can only hope to be that sort of "light" in someone else's life! I've been at this "nowhere station" for quite some time. Waiting, idling, hoping, doing I don't really know what. But now, now I'm leaving here, I'm walking away. It took me a long time to realise that there was no train coming. I don't know where I'm headed, or what the future holds – hopefully, good health and success! But as I walk, I walk with faith and hope alongside me and the loving gaze of Allah as He watches over me …!

Mrs Independent

Quraisha Dawood

"Say yes to him," the aunty urges.

I know she isn't saying this because she knows him or that she thinks I will be happy with him. She says this because she doesn't think I will have another chance at getting married. To her, my family is dysfunctional. I am the girl nobody will want to marry. Growing up as an only child of a single parent household has taught me certain things. These "things" I did not ask to learn, but life taught them to me anyway. Ultimately I have learnt that everyone, even those in the darkest places, have choices. Some will choose to pity, other will choose to provoke and then there are those who will choose to prove themselves, like my mother. She could have relaxed into a life of arranged conveniences, but instead she chose to face the world head on and alone. But life has also taught me that there is a big difference between being alone and being lonely. We were never lonely. We laughed, we went on holidays, and we made the best of our two member family. Thanks to her education, independence and above all, a resilient faith in the Almighty, her life has not been easy, but she can proudly say she accomplished every triumph on her own – and looked good doing it. And this, for me, does not spell out dysfunction. In fact, many of my friends admired her for not choosing to stay married for the fear of "what people will say". Of course there are those who continue to judge a professional Muslim woman for being unmarried as if she is half a human being, and let them. They will forever be imprisoned in their own minds.

I never thought I would get married. I wasn't the typical Muslim girl. I was a shade darker than most. I wore unbranded clothing. I took the bus. I was that shy girl in school and university who succumbed to dullness in the shadows of the sparkly girls. They radiated charm, unlike awkward, nerdy me. Somehow I found my niche in writing poetry, a blog, feature articles, and political cartoons. My confidence grew as I grew. I did experience the odd heartbreak now and then. They were dramatic and short-lived and they are now safely hidden in the box labeled "what was I thinking?" I'm sure there are a few grey hairs on my mother's head that will attest to that time. Of course, there were one or two "arranged" meetings my family or friends engineered, because as a *Memon* girl of twenty-three, I was nearing my sell-by date and I was told the elders were starting to "worry". I didn't particularly enjoy parading around for would-be suitors or their parents like a bejeweled circus elephant, but I didn't completely rule out this option. Settling for someone wasn't an option either. I wasn't going to say yes to someone just because people thought he was a good catch or that it was time for me to get married. But I did want to spend my life with someone. All I knew was that he had to have an amazing smile. I didn't necessarily go out to prove that I was marriage material, but I prayed for someone who would be perfect for me to come along when the time was right.

And in between becoming a hard-working academic and an independent individual, the right man found me. Actually, we knew each other for a year before we realised that we were each other's missing puzzle pieces. He was tall and handsome in a way he is still unaware of. And yes, he had a smile that can rival the sun's warmth and dimples that you could store spare change in. But most of all, he was kind, humble, romantic and extremely witty. We were engaged for a year before we married in January 2010.

Marriage is a strange concept. I remember waking up on the quiet morning after our wedding and thinking, "Okay so now I have a man in my bed. Forever?" Granted, he was and is the man of my dreams, but for someone who is used to being alone most of the time, it was all new territory. Literally. From seeing my family the next day to wrapping my tongue around the word "husband", it was an awkward time. Moving into our new flat wasn't just playing house – it was growing up. I missed my mother. Thankfully she was only one building away, but I had never lived with a man. I felt compelled to be the perfect Stepford-wife version of myself. But after a month or two, I found myself relaxing into the word "wife". I liked it. Mine and his became "ours". While I wasn't the queen of the kitchen before I got married (potato fry was the first meal I cooked for him), I was excited by the concept of creating something from scratch for him. I tried new recipes, sometimes relying on my instincts and excelled in these culinary adventures. The first time I made butter chicken, he said, "My word. Your mom needs to try this!" (Insert imaginary gold star on forehead here). Cooking wasn't work – it became an expression of my love for him. And I really do love the moments I spend with him.

The awkwardness in the beginning seems silly now. Perhaps I had felt that being married meant that I couldn't be independent. Perhaps, I felt I would lose too much of myself in letting him take care of me. But the balance lies in letting someone care for you while still retaining your own identity. In being the same assertive girl he fell in love with three years ago, and embracing this new gift.

Now, I am more me than I have ever been. I have completed my Masters degree, I am a PhD candidate and he has travelled with me to Europe on conference. Balancing all of this isn't a walk in the park. There are days when I would like to have a butler on call, who makes my chores disappear. Or days when I wish I could just get some retail therapy. It is good to feel these things. I wouldn't like to be a robot. Most of the time, time management allows me to find a way to "do me" during the day and "do us" when he is home. I'm sure I will humbly eat these words when we have children.

But marriage is not all fairytale. I remember sitting with my friends at university discussing our ideal lives and in our teenage Bollywood delirium, we all thought we would have the perfect lives when we were married. I wish I could go back and tell myself to live in the moment … and also that I should stop wearing those "funky" blue shoes. Happiness like this comes around once in a lifetime. But it brings with it adult problems our minds couldn't fathom back then. There are serious talks to be had about finances and family. Whether we like it or not, these are never truly going to go away. I love him for his loyalty. We are very different people in some ways. He grew up seeing extended family almost every other day while I saw mine on *Eid* days. He wanted a big wedding, including everyone in his life, and I wanted a small one with only those who deserved to be there. In being an extremely private person, I was not and still am not used to seeing family often and having them have an opinion about the way I live. Perhaps one day when I am a granny I will reach that point and my kids can tire of seeing me. But for now, it is an issue we work around. Sometimes I struggle with being the "dutiful daughter-in-law", and the expectations that come with it, but I am the best I can be. He is the type of person who will forgive and accept and I am the type who will cut someone out of my life if they don't add to it. I learn from his tolerance. He learns to draw lines in the sand.

Together, we find the balance. Ultimately, we trust each other. Within this, we find freedom. That's where the beauty of my marriage lies. I am the dreamer, and he is the realist. I hurt with my words. He is more forgiving. I am fire. He is coolness. He gives me the freedom to be creative, to be emotional and to be alone when I need it (and I don't give him any freedom at all).

I write this as I wait for him to return from work. I add cinnamon to the butternut mash. Marriage is like that. He is my cinnamon. He adds a sweetness to me that was never there. I will always need him. In this lifetime or the next, I will choose him over and over again. For in this space next to him, in the curve of his arm, I am that girl who sparkles.

Only He as my Creator is the best of all planners!

Sumaya Kola

In my childhood years, I dreamt of being the "A" student, travelling the world and becoming a strong independent young woman. I am different now, to how I was back then … My twenty-five years of living have made me more spiritually inclined. Each life lesson has made me stronger and wiser. I went from being the overachieving perfectionist to wanting the simple things in life, the things that normal people take for granted – just to breathe and live and to enjoy each day to its fullest.

As a child I made a promise to myself that I would never marry … I grew up in a home where I watched my mother being abused time and time again by a drug addicted father. They divorced when I was five years old after which I was raised by my mother who always showed a strong and independent face to my sister and me. When I was 10, my mother re-married, only to be hurt again and then divorced once again nine years later. If someone would have asked me, back then, what my hopes for the future were, I would normally tell them that my hope was to complete school, go to medical school, become a cardiologist, go off to work in London and raise an adopted child on my own … Marriage was not on my "bucket list" but … things change, dreams change and people change.

When I was 14 years old I was diagnosed with a rare medical condition known as Pulmonary Hypertension (PH). PH is the term used when the blood pressure in the lungs rises up to abnormal levels, causing damage to the delicate blood vessels which in turn puts pressure on the heart to work harder and faster in order to supply the muscles of the body with sufficient oxygen in order to function. There was no sudden change in my outlook on life after being diagnosed with PH. In fact my perspective on life remained normal for many years thereafter and it was only with time that I slowly began the process of change.

After completing school and no longer the naïve, ignorant girl that I once was, I knew that life was serious business. I wasn't sure what I wanted to do or where I was going to, I just knew that I had to find my way. I wasn't sure whether I wanted to study or not, let alone what to study. I still was not serious about marriage and so every man that showed interest in me, I pushed away. This, I feel, was one of the most dark and complicated periods of my life. Funny enough the confusion had little to do with my illness.

About two years ago my health began deteriorating. I knew that the change would happen but I was not ready for it. I was told that my heart was not coping and that I would need a heart/lung transplant, but I was shattered to hear that I possibly would not be able to live a normal life. The doctors explained the intricate details of my condition and expected future. They explained that they were aware that I would be considering marriage but that there were limitations to my abilities both sexually and physically. Any prospective Mr Eligible, whoever he was, would need to be told about my condition. I would not be able to carry a child or have a normal intimate relationship with a man, considering the fact that my lungs were damaged. The words sunk in like daggers carving ice – sharp and cold … and I suddenly realised the desperate need that gnawed deep into my flesh to find my life companion, settle down and have a family. Tears streamed down my face as the black reality of the situation hit me hard.

Which man would want to be with woman who was sick? Which man would want to be with a woman who could not live a normal intimate life with him? Which man would want to be with a woman who would give him no children?

Nine months ago, I was told that the time for me to be listed for a heart transplant has come. At first I experienced anxiety to the extent of losing hope. I wallowed in self-pity over things that I had not done. I then realised giving up did nothing for me and if I wanted to fulfil my hopes and dreams, I needed to fight in order to survive. I have also learned how to put my full faith in Allah and hand my life over to *Him* completely. I have learned that I am stronger than I think I am and most of all, I have learned to never give up hope: there is goodness in everything no matter how bad it seems. My faith in Allah and the help of my transplant psychologist have taught me how to let go, especially of the things that you cannot control. This, I feel, is one of the most important lessons I need to carry with me through my illness, the transplant and my life thereafter. I feel that hope has replaced the fear that was strangling me. I look forward to the day that I will be able to breathe easy and live a normal life again. The lesson of letting go has also helped me deal with my hopes of getting married. Marriage, like everything else in life, is something out of one's control. I have realised that when the right person comes along, somebody who will accept me as I am, I will marry, and perhaps my story will be a "happily ever after" and perhaps it will not … but *shukr Alhamdullilah*, I have learnt to have faith and trust in Allah because only *He* as my *Creator* is the best of all planners.

My ideal partner

Sumayya Mehtar

I often encounter questions relating to marriage both from family members and from complete strangers. They want to know when I will marry and what I seek in a marriage partner. I usually brush off these questions with a smile or simply reply by saying I will marry one day, Allah willing. I ponder a lot about my *taqdeer*, about where my destiny will take me. I wonder about the qualities I would like in a husband and why I would want those qualities. Yesterday, I was unsure but today … after much thought and deliberation I have decided that I would like my future husband to have the same personality and characteristics as my father. I firmly do believe that Allah, in my father, has given me the perfect example of how a husband should be, so when I find him I know that I will immediately recognise and connect with him.

My father has four unique personality traits that I would want my future husband to possess. First is kindness, genuine kindness. Second is intelligence, so that when both of us have left our prime we can still make each other laugh. Third is being responsible and accepting all that comes along with being a husband and father. The fourth and most important trait is having an unbiased, fair nature and displaying a fine example of gender equality within the home.

I said my husband has to be kind, but not in the generic sense of the term. He has to be willing to inconvenience himself to make something better than when he left it and without expecting any compensation. My father is certainly a fine example of this trait. Throughout his life he has assisted many people from all walks of life. I am told that my family was in an unstable financial situation during the first few years of my life, but mum relates that then too my father would assist people who were in a worse off situation than himself. My father is a philanthropist who assists the poor and uplifts the underprivileged communities of Malawi. I only realised the extent of his efforts when I undertook to visit Malawi a year ago. I felt proud to be my father's daughter.

As a humble man, my father never discussed his projects with the family. It was always a subject that he kept to himself. He always says what the right hand gives the left hand shouldn't know. In Malawi, the beautiful scene of hundreds of eager students from poor impoverished backgrounds speaking Arabic, reading and writing and memorising the *Quran* brought tears to my eyes. My father believes that the foundation of every state is the education of its youth and has therefore contributed to the education of many underprivileged and orphaned kids. Giving to the poor is a quality which I have adopted from my father and *Insha'Allah* my future husband would display the same. Aameen.

I value intelligence in a prospective marriage partner because my father was both intelligent and humble. Pride and arrogance is not a part of my father's nature and hence he taught me to be humble and simple. My father always said that pride is a quality for Allah Almighty alone and that pride and arrogance diminishes wisdom. I want my prospective marriage partner to give me an opinion about an article he read in the newspaper or to provide new light on some current event. As I am one of those vivacious, bold characters always analysing newspaper articles, commenting on various blogs, and observing human behaviour, I would prefer having a partner that shares the same interests and at the same time respects my thoughts and opinions. Perhaps it is pertinent to mention here that my father did not complete his formal education. However, having started out from humble beginnings he eventually became a successful businessman. Sir Francis Bacon once said, "Reading maketh a full man, conference a ready man, and writing an exact man." My father has always encouraged my brother and me to acquire knowledge through reading. It is through excessive reading of the newspaper that my father had acquired his knowledge in finances and the stock exchange. Hence, being successful is definitely not dependent on a formal theoretical school education. It is dependent upon perseverance and striving towards achieving a goal. Education is all around us. Every day we educate ourselves and learn new things through the people with whom we meet and interact. Whilst most middle aged people of today are not very familiar with computers and the latest technology, I'm quite proud to say that my father is computer literate and is in fact an avid "Facebooker". Of course my mother gets annoyed with the fact that the whole world knows she is ill or is leaving on a vacation but my friends and colleagues on the other hand find it quite hilarious that my father is pretty much in tune with the times.

The third characteristic that I crave in a marriage partner is one that all the other qualities branch from – responsibility. Responsibility is something that makes us who we are. How someone handles responsibility undoubtedly determines their honour. A sense of responsibility is also something that is achieved through numerous experiences and over a considerable period of time. Ambition in one's career is certainly not something that comes before Allah, family and friends. No matter what you've done for yourself or for humanity, if you can't look back on having given love and attention to your own family, what have you really accomplished? My husband should put our religion first, then the values that are important to me will also be important to him.

My father often tells me stories of him being the youngest child, growing up in a large household of nine children – with seven brothers and two sisters. From a young age, my father and his siblings took on responsibilities to help their father provide for the family's basic needs. My late *Daada* was the principal of a school and on a teacher's salary, he did not manage to provide fully for his large family. My *Daada* was also not the type of a man who was business orientated and neither was he ambitious. He was a man of Allah, purely content with passing on the knowledge he possessed to the children who he taught. Despite facing hardships and difficulties, my father and his siblings were never really deprived of anything. It was as though Allah Almighty was there to watch over them and fulfill all their needs and desires. Together they always managed to make ends meet at the end of every month that passed. My father always says that hard work has never killed anyone and hence he has been working from a young age of fifteen. Forty years later, he stills continues to work and is now the chairman of his own company.

For an expression that is much talked about, you rarely come across a clear definition of what gender equality actually means. I'm pretty sure different people mean very different things when talking about gender equality, and many people probably are not aware of exactly what they mean. Gender equality can be defined as the measurable equal representation of women and men. Gender equality does not imply that women and men are the same, but that they have equal value and should be accorded equal treatment. The concept of gender equality is very important to me and my future husband will have to understand that whilst males and females have different roles and responsibilities within a home, I will be an equal partner to him. Despite being brought up in a traditional[i] Indian Muslim home that is very religiously inclined, my father is a man of liberal thought and broad vision. Hence, the same opportunities given to my brother were afforded to me as well. My *Daada* did not allow my *Foois* to pursue studies or progress into a career path. There was an ideology in most Indian Muslim homes during those times whereby it was frowned upon for a woman to seek an education, pursue a career path and become a productive member of society. The norm was for fathers to take their daughters out of school after completing grade 7 or 10, find them suitors and get them married. Many of these women formed identities in relation to those who they were dependent on. For many, cooking and nurturing many children became their sport. Their lives would be spent trying to cope with mother's in-law and sister's in-law issues in an extended household.

Whilst the drama still continues for some Muslim women, up to today, the dynamics of most Muslim women growing up within traditional homes have changed somewhat over the last decade. My own personal experiences are definitely a fine example of this metamorphosis in Muslim society. My father has always supported me in my career path and I was also allowed to travel the world alone. During my high school years, I was allowed to go on weekend camping trips and I participated in various types of activities that would have been frowned upon had I been born two decades earlier.

Euripides, a Greek playwright once said, "Experience travel – these are as education in themselves." Traveling was also a great *sunnah* and very much a part of the Prophet Muhammad's (*SAW*) lifestyle. He traveled far and wide in search of knowledge and to spread Islam. Throughout my life my father has encouraged us to travel and interact with different people from all walks of life. It is through this liberal upbringing that I have managed to break through norms and boundaries and view the many facets of life through the eyes of individuals from different cultural and religious backgrounds. The "me" who left South Africa four years ago to expand my pharmaceutical knowledge is certainly not the same "me" I am currently. I have changed in the many different aspects of my life, from my dressing to my thinking.

Reflecting on who I have become, I have found that growing up in South Africa has shielded me from the lives of others around the world. I have thus developed an almost elite identity in believing that my lifestyle as a practicing Muslim is the best and all other sects are wrong. When I set foot in the Middle East a few years ago, I was surprised to be interacting and working with people from many different Islamic sects. Whilst there are significant variations in many of these sects, I was astounded at the good character and humble qualities displayed by many individuals who belonged to these varying sects. We are all Muslim and although some of our ways may differ, we all fulfill our religious obligations to the best of our abilities and for the pleasure of Allah alone.

In finding the new "me" my dressing also changed. After interacting with European and American women who had been ostracised and harassed for wearing a headscarf, I began understanding the value of covering my hair as part of my identity as a Muslim woman. I felt proud to be a Muslim woman and I realised how fortunate women are in South Africa, to be allowed to wear a head scarf or face veil with complete freedom without being harassed by any governmental authority. On my travels through various parts of the world, I have been stopped by fellow passengers or individuals who would enquire about my head scarf. I understood these moments as a perfect opportunity for me to be instrumental in introducing these people to my religion and also to try to change their perceptions about being Muslim. Prior to leaving for the Middle East I was the retail pharmacy manager for a well known private hospital in South Africa. I wore suits and formal clothing to compliment my stylish hair cut. My father advised me on various issues and topics but did not force me to do anything with which I was not comfortable. My father believes that change and guidance comes from Allah alone. He also believes that it is dangerous to bring up children with one tracked minds. My father always reiterates that whilst we should have a firm Islamic background, it is imperative that we embrace other peoples' cultures and religions. My father encouraged me to learn about Christianity, Judaism, Hinduism or any other religion for that matter. The rationale behind this, he said, is that when others question our religion, we will be better informed to answer such questions. My father is right. This is the way of Islam and this is how the pioneers of Islam approached their religion.

I have not yet discussed the physical characteristics of my ideal partner because for me, this is not what I yearn for. He can have blonde hair and green eyes and be three inches shorter than me or he can be bald and be a foot taller than me. I do not care. I do not know what the future holds for me, or where my destiny will take me, but I do know the support a husband offers a wife and a wife to her husband is a part of life's fulfillment. So, I wait patiently until the time comes for Allah Almighty to reveal his master plan for me. Until then I will remain committed to my top four priorities because I know with certainty that I am on the right path to finding my ideal partner.

Run, samoosa, run

Anonymous

My weekend began whilst baking a batch of heart-shaped biscuits, when my mother told me that there would be a Mr Eligible coming to see me. I was rightfully angry for not being told earlier. "How could you not tell me?" I yelled, staring at the heart-shaped biscuits which had "desperation" written all over them. Mother, who had obviously read my thoughts, replied, "You are only eighteen, my dear. Who would consider you desperate?" It was obvious that the situation was stressing my mother out too.

My parents often debated the possibility of allowing a Mr Eligible to come to see me, mainly due to what family members and friends had told them. I was the first of my siblings and cousins to attend university … and this often resulted in uncomfortable lectures from my *Khalas* and *Foois* about how Mr Eligible would find my "degrees" intimidating, how my studies would postpone marriage and in turn would lead "the people" to think that there was something wrong with me.

I panicked at the thought of Mr Eligible coming to see me. My first concern was the pimples that erupt on my face whenever I experience the slightest stress. I needed to mix my favourite *chana flour* face mask and gently spread it over my face in preparation for the grand visit. I also needed to wax my moustache, extended side burns and goatee. Whilst I may have inherited fair skin from my *Surtee* ancestors, I also was bestowed with the dreaded "Indian chick" hairiness. All of this activity kept my mind busy and everybody steered clear of me and my irritable mood.

Fast forward … Saturday afternoon. I remember being too nervous to eat lunch – the staple of *khuri kitchree.* I stressed about what to wear. I decided on a dark chocolate velvet dress that sat snug around my curves but was decent enough to pass the maybe future mother-in-law's "judging" eyes.

My *Khala* arrived with two platters of savouries. She brought her three children with her, who together with my younger siblings created enough mayhem to keep the visit from becoming awkward.

We set the tables separately, for men and women. My mother used her favourite dinner service and the embroidered table cloth with matching napkins, which she had brought back from a trip to *Makkah*, usually reserved for *Eid*. Plates were laden with sweet and spicy finger foods, hot and cold drinks and a selection of mini cakes and desserts. Even though the tables were set, my *Khala* insisted that I carry a tray as according to tradition so that Mr Eligible and his mother could have a full view of me. This tradition did not suit me especially since my hands shake when I am nervous. My parents understood my fear and I did not carry the tray – the tradition had been bypassed in my honour. *Shukr Alhamdullilah*!

I don't remember much about their arrival or sitting and practicing the fine and ridiculous art of making small talk with absolute strangers, who held over me the power of approval or rejection. I needed to portray myself as having a functioning brain without sounding like a "smartass". For me, this task was important. I remembered and referred to an article I had once read that provided advice for handling a job interview. The article covered everything from what not to wear, to conveying confidence through your body language, what questions to ask, and which not to. In hindsight, it was this article that helped me on that day.

Everything was going smoothly, that is until someone announced that there were two brothers that had come to see me. What?! Who does that? How does that work? I'm sure all this must have shown on my face, because I caught their mother looking at me strangely. Or maybe it was my oversensitive ego … Then came crunch time! "Personal interview". I was expecting this, but hearing it out loud somewhat scared me.

We trooped to my bedroom, my good self, the eldest brother and the go-between aunty, who lived one street away and was Mr Eligible's *Fooi*. Aunty Shireen introduced us. We stood in the only free space in my room, a one by one and a half metre gap between my bed and the closet. I don't remember his name probably because I was stressing over where to sit. Would the bed seem suggestive? Eventually I maneuvered my way to the low dressing table, where I promptly threw open the window, despite the chilly

June afternoon, and propped one foot on the base of the bed, striving for elegance.

I must have succeeded because Aunty Shireen said, "I'm going to leave you two to get to know one another."

She then looked at Mr Eligible and said, "She's a good girl. You won't find her standing on the street corner."

She left and shut the door behind her. Silence. We sat quietly. I think we examined everything from the pleats on the curtain to the fine crack running down the wall adjacent to my door, the result of one too many slams. Predictably we both spoke at the same time and again asked the other to go first, laughed and continued talking for almost an hour. He was cute in an "Indian boy way" – with a thin beanpole physique, dark brown eyes, naturally spiky hair, and a closely cropped beard. He wore formal pants, a shirt and a knitted vest. He was an accountant.

"Do you always wear the headscarf?" he asked. "Or is it just because you just came back from *Hajj*?" I laughed, striving for husky rather than nervous and high pitched. "Now would be a good time to tell you that I have started wearing *purdah*."

There was a horrified look on his face. "I mean I sometimes step out of the house, forgetting to wear it, but I am trying to," I explained.

"At work we have functions and I would like my wife to dress up for it. Would you remove your scarf for such a thing?" he asked. I remember thinking if his question was meant to test me. I smiled sweetly and replied, "I've been wearing the headscarf since I was twelve and therefore I think it's safe to say no. That won't be happening." And that was the end of that. The second brother did not ask to speak to me which left me relieved.

My second *samoosa* run turned out as the first – he was not my type and he did not come back. Some say it's the third time lucky rule … when I saw the third contender, I hoped with all my heart that this was him. He looked like everything I never wanted and ever wanted. He was a mere head taller than myself (never wanted), had the sweetest dark eyes and long lashes that belonged on a girl (ever wanted), and a couple of days' worth stubble on a very cute face (I had no idea until then how much I liked a beard, not a Santa Claus kind, but a one-that-acknowledged-he-was-a-guy kind …) and he wore clean takkies! I must have looked at his shoes a lot, because he thought I was having very naughty thoughts right there. I do however claim absolute innocence … they were just so clean!

I decided to ask my older brother to sit with us which turned out to be a big mistake. I was too embarrassed to ask any of my usual questions with my brother being present, which resulted in my brother asking *the* most epically weird ones on my behalf, and embarrassing me!

My brother asked, "Do you eat *roti*?" and when Mr Eligible shook his head, a little dazed (I mean who would ever see that coming as a starter question?), my big brother chortled, "Good, because my little sister can't make them to save her life."

My brother then extended a pack of cigarettes and asked, "You smoke?"

He continued, "How often would you bring her home to visit? Would you be okay with her continuing her studies? She is becoming a teacher, it would be advisable to let her continue, and it would benefit your children."

I don't remember if Mr Eligible replied. I remember my face burning a deep red in embarrassment. In hindsight however, those were probably *the* most important questions because questions regarding tastes in food and movies can be ambiguous.

This was the shortest "get to know each other" of the three, and I fully expected not to hear from him again. It made me sad when the Mr Eligibles did not come back. I felt as though there was something deeply wrong with me. To help get my mind off of these "samoosa runs", I went for a holiday to my grandparents. My *Nanima* insisted I learn how to roll the perfect *roti*. To her surprise, I managed the perfect outline of Africa using a dinner plate and a knife. The following Monday, Mr Eligible Number Three's grandmother, who is my *Naana*'s first cousin, called. My grandparents did not say anything and in sadness I assumed that Mr Eligible did not like me.

A week later, during our journey home from my grandparents, my father told me that the family of Mr Eligible Number Three had proposed. So as a condensed version of events: between exams,

"Aunty Rosie" and a series of confusing *istikhara salaahs*, I gave my answer.

A month later we held an informal engagement which involved me being force-fed sweet meats and him being offered vinegar spiked juice. A date was set for the *nikah*, and a month and a half later after an exchange of gold chains and wrist watches, I was married …

My Samoosa Express to finding my soul mate

Fatima Adam

I am a young Muslim lady and this is my story, carved in stone and written from the depths of my heart. If I can say so myself, I am an amazing young woman and those who have taken the time to get to know me would pay testimony to the stark honesty in my self-analysis. Wherever I went as a single young woman, people would enquire about me. They would ask if I were married, my age and whether I was interested in getting married. Others made assumptions about me based on my outward appearance and they drew conclusions about me based on their perceptions of my life.

I had a difficult childhood and as I grew up I chose to show a positive front to the public regardless of what I felt. After I had matriculated I registered at university with the aim of gaining an education that would allow me to be an independent woman. As I persevered through university I became a confident and assertive woman. Many people in the community commented that I was arrogant and some would even say, "You have a big mouth, just wait, you are going to get a husband who is going to fix you up!"

Very often I would walk away and cry as I couldn't understand why people managed to see only the negative end of my comments. My mother always pleaded with me to keep quiet and just smile like all the other young girls did, because that's what men wanted, sweet and polite girls. My response to that was, "In that case I won't be getting married."

My pursuit of education challenged the conventional perception of a Muslim wife. My thoughts revolved around the fact that women should be heard. A vociferous and confident woman does not necessarily have to be a bad woman. My opinion was often that the quiet woman suffered silently inside and it was better to speak about things rather than just accept them. Islamic society had suppressed women. I understood the role of women in Islam and I read about the Prophet Muhammad's wives and how strong they were. I read about Khadija (*RA*) who was a successful and wealthy businesswoman. Undeterred by her position, Prophet Muhammad saw the strength within her and recognised that she would be an amazing wife. This historical story became my inspiration and I promised myself that I would not settle for anything less. I knew that it would not be easy to find someone who would allow me to be myself.

At university I was exposed to the different types of young men out there in the Muslim community – including those who portrayed themselves as respectful young men to their parents, yet while at university they behaved like unruly hooligans. I witnessed these "respectful young men" taking drugs, alcohol and pursuing short-term relationships with non-Muslim women. I often found myself in the company of these people but I knew my boundaries. My social engagements with these young men and women at university gave me a clear insight into the expectations of what each wanted in a partner. The girls wanted rich men, who would provide them with a life of luxury and comfort. The men wanted beautiful women who would choose to put their lives on hold and constantly seek to address their husband's needs. I could not relate to that. Some of my friends married while they were at university, but not me. Note that not all the young men were unruly, there were those men who were engrossed in their studies and chose not to socialise much. I wondered about these young men. I wondered about their goals in life and what their experiences were in life that made them career-driven. I often wanted to strike up a conversation with these young men but I felt self-conscious and would choose not to for fear of being embarrassed.

I was in my mid twenties and family members and members of the community expressed concern about my lack of interest in marriage. They therefore took it upon themselves to find me a suitor. My mother always encouraged me and would advise me to give the young men opportunity to come over with their families. "This could be the beginning of a good relationship," my mother would say. The problem was that I didn't think that a personal relationship could begin under such stressful circumstances. Anyway, I succumbed to the pressure and soon lost count of the number of young men that came for tea to "see". It always started by a family friend knowing of a young man who was "looking for a good girl". When I turned their choice of Mr Eligible down, I was no longer the "good girl" because I had "hurt" someone's ego.

I often wondered how people could think that they were helping you when they bring an entire family to see you. That was not help; that was torment. I questioned whether people understood the stress placed upon me in preparation for the "samoosa express". I stressed about my looks and what to wear – headscarf or no headscarf? I pondered on what to say and on how to enter. Mother and I needed to make decisions regarding what to serve with tea – samoosas and cake, or just dried fruit and sweets. We finally decided that our choice of treats depended on whether we liked the Mr Eligible or not. Yes, we were sneaky, but the stress was awful. What a way to destroy a young woman's self-esteem.

As the number of people who came along grew, I noticed a trend; most of the young men did not have the confidence to speak for themselves. Often the parents chose to do the talking. The young man would sit there looking down until I asked a question. When it was time for us to go and speak for a short while on our own, I witnessed the miraculous metamorphosis of a so-called innocent boy to a raving club DJ. Often the young man would speak in a manner that I saw at university, using lingo that was far from English. "Did he think that this would impress me?" I often asked myself. He would flash out his latest cell phone and ask for my number, which I refused to give. There was also the curiosity of the family members. They would all call to enquire what I thought, was I going to marry him? How do you decide to marry someone if he shows you two different personalities in a span of thirty minutes?

Once a young man's mother was so eager for me to marry her son that she called me to tell me that they had decided to buy a BMW for me. I just had to accept the proposal and I would receive the car keys on the engagement day. I was appalled by this. "Do they think I am that cheap? I do not need money and fame."

At the next incident with another young man I was promised a fully furnished house. Often I would receive expensive gifts from the young man who visited in the hope that material gifts would win me over. I didn't know what exactly I wanted in a man but I knew that the day I met the man I would know it.

I was fortunate to have a few friends that could relate to my life as they experienced similar incidents. I often chatted to my friends about these peculiar visits and at one stage we tried to take count of the number of people that had come to meet us. We laughed and realised that we had lost count. At one time a friend and I realised that there was one young man that had gone to see both of us. We took the opportunity to compare notes and shared a giggle about our experiences. Only my friends knew how stressful the meetings were.

I eventually decided not to have anyone come over to see me. I was in the final year of receiving a master's degree and I planned to graduate and go overseas. I was excited by the new prospects but my idea was met with great criticism from my family. Everyone wanted me to get married. I often felt that I could not bring myself to settle for a partner who did not speak to my heart. I did not want money; I wanted a "mature" man who could engage confidently in conversation. I wanted a responsible man. Why was it so difficult to find a person like that?

At that point I received a call from a family friend asking me to meet another young man. At first I refused, but feeling pressured I agreed to meet him. I did not make much effort in my dressing. When the doorbell rang, my mother answered the door; it was him and his aunt, nobody else. He was going to do the talking. His aunt left us alone, and yes, it was the beginning of a new relationship. My heart spoke at the mere sight of him and after engaging in conversation and observing his demeanour and character I knew that he was the one. I didn't feel pressured. He allowed me to talk and conversed in turn and to this day, *Alhamdullilah,* we continue chatting with our children beside us.

Hope, love, faith

Bibi-aisha Wadvalla

In the summer of '98, with the heady unburdened hopes of youth, we thought we could plan our futures. It was a hazy, summer evening, the kind that leaves you in a soporific stupor. In an old farmhouse in a small country town, I struck upon an idea to pass the time. My three sisters and I would each write down where we saw each other in five and ten years' time. We were eighteen, sixteen, fifteen and thirteen years old at the time. We resolved to bury the book, and not open it until each period passed. Years went by; some predictions were spot on, while in other ways we didn't follow our expected paths.

Fourteen years have since become memories, and the book has disappeared. I still remember most of what we wrote, the weighty words of our own dreams and expectations that were foisted on us. Between us, we've achieved most of what we aimed for, and more. But one assumedly natural event continues to elude us; the prospect of which is inversely proportional to age.

We are girl-women, captured in a limbo of lost dreams.

Like most Indian women, I look younger than my age. Most people subtract four years, while some (bless them) take off as many as eight. So when I meet new people, and the age question is asked, I'm invariably amused or annoyed by the reactions.

"No!" they exclaim. "But you look so young." Amusing.

"Oh my, but why aren't you married?" Annoying.

But regardless of the reaction, there's that awkward moment when the pity is tangible. I'm thirty. And I'm single. Never married. No, I'm not too fussy, nor too career-minded, nor so unappealing that nobody has ever wanted to marry me. I've been told that I expect too much, that I'm too independent and ambitious, and it's been implied there must be something wrong with me. I didn't mind it when I was in my mid-twenties, and still feel comfortable with my single status. But it irks me to be judged according to society's narrow norms.

Unlike most of my peers, I never wanted to marry young. At fourteen, my Accounting teacher rudely dismissed my intention to marry at twenty-four. "You'll be married at eighteen," she sneered. At twenty-four, still unmarried, fate called me to Egypt. In Cairo, my soul and intellect were nourished; and a soothing balm of contentment dissipated the angst of preceding years. But in that cocoon, a niggling fear ate at me. I felt responsible for my failure to meet my goal of being married at twenty-four, and worried that I had discarded opportunities of marriage. And through that doubt, I came to truly believe in the *qadr* of Allah, in the power of faith and God's Will. I look back at my experiences and the choices I made, and I'm assured I tied my camel [iv]. It's a long-standing and quite common sentiment that women go to university to find husbands. While some women candidly admit to this, it's an unfair slur against those who truly wish to practise in the field they study. For both men and women though, there's an expectation that the heart and not only the brain will be stimulated, and that marriage to a love partner discovered on campus will immediately follow graduation. When I went to university, aunts and cousins would often ask if I'd met anyone on campus, and my answer became a predictable "no". Over the years, there were declarations of love. I had friends tell me I was the type of girl they could see themselves marrying, but I didn't meet anyone I could see myself marrying. I endured two *samoosa* runs – that antiquated ritual, which is the epitome of awkwardness. In both cases, we experienced a mutual lack of compatibility. Due to my adherence to *hijab*, people assume I'm "homely". I'm adept at keeping a home, but I don't see myself being solely a housewife. There were numerous offers of interest, with the record being eight in five months when I was twenty-three. I seriously considered one offer from my friend's brother who reiterated his desire to marry me. Despite getting along well with his family, and my family thinking well of him; and despite thinking he'd make a good husband, I just couldn't see myself as his wife. A few months later, he met someone who returned his affections, and they remain happily married.

After a few months in Cairo, I questioned if, indeed, I was too fussy; if I expected impossible qualities in a husband; if I was wrong in not praying *istikharah* for every guy who was interested. I turned to my *halqah* teacher for advice, who assured me I had not sabotaged *taqdeer*. One of my flatmates, a clinical psychologist, told me I was looking for someone who possessed similar qualities to my own. I said I was looking for someone who is more than I am, but yet is my equal.

I met him four years later.

At the start of 2010, in Cairo, my flat mates and I threw a house-warming/New Year's party, the theme being Hope. We asked guests to dress in colours that reflected their hopes for the year. My hope was for love. I hoped for an all-encompassing love which would embrace all areas of my life. I wore a peach-coloured silk shirt underneath a red coat. Red for passion, excitement, energy. Peach for calmness, love, wisdom. I returned to South Africa for a vacation at the end of May, at the start of winter. To me, it felt like spring. The lushness of hope whispered of serendipity. And at the end of winter, fate intervened. It wasn't a random, unplanned meeting, but it was fortuitous in that I had almost changed my mind about going out that night. A thought struck me while talking to him, "This is a boy I can take home to meet my parents." I shrugged it off, mocking the workings of my mind. Besides, he was too young for me. Three months later, he was the first guy I took home to meet my parents formally. But I'm jumping ahead. After having coffee together that night, we bumped into each other a few weeks later, in another city. We chatted briefly. Slowly, we started communicating online, but casually, as friends. He visited Cairo two months after we first met. While showing him around, I realised I was interested. I sensed interest on his side, too. Two weeks later, I made *duah*, "Oh, Allah, if he is good for me, and if he likes me too, then let him tell me he wants to get to know me for the purpose of marriage." The next day, he called to say just that. And so we embarked on "a form of courtship", as he so quaintly phrased it. We lived in different countries and so spent hours talking on the phone everyday and emailing and messaging. It was all surreal in that we were discussing the future, how many children to have, when to have them, how to raise them, possible countries to live in for work/graduate studies, how often we'd see our families weekly, thoughts on entertaining guests, socialising, religious ideology and a whole bunch of other stuff, right at the beginning. It was a serious attempt at determining our compatibility for marriage, religiously and socially. Naturally, there needed to be chemistry too. And there was.

I prayed *istikhara* from the outset, not wanting my personal desires to influence me. And within a few weeks, we both felt quite certain of sharing a life together. However, this was not the perfect love story. I wasn't insulted when he told me that his mother said I was too old, on the shelf. At twenty-eight, to me this was a clichéd viewpoint that the community continued to flounder under. But it pinched to hear she thought I was single because nobody else wanted to marry me, and that I was controlling him. It made me aware of a weakness in my supposed immunity to the viral probing behind why I wasn't married. I felt a need to defend myself against the untruth. He assured me that he had told her of my past suitors. "You should have said I'm single because I've been waiting for someone like you," I teased.

I had anticipated his parents wouldn't be pleased when they heard he wanted to marry me. A five-year age gap, where the girl is older, is sure to raise a few eyebrows in society. But I naively thought they'd meet me and grow to like me, or at least just accept me. What I could not have imagined was the distilled distaste, the vehement wrath which would pour forth. I was disappointed when I was told of their objections, and ashamedly, for a brief moment, felt disillusionment of faith. But that was swiftly vanquished. *Tawakkul Allah* – in Allah I trust. For a few days I floundered, wondering if he and I should continue the relationship. I prayed *istikharah* again, and all doubts disappeared. And in the midst of an uprising for freedom and human rights, my heart was breaking its own shackles. On a day when Egypt raged, when all communication was shut down, when I choked on tear gas and ducked to evade bullets, when I numbly witnessed police brutality; my heart exulted, for it had fallen in love.

For him, the feelings these events evoked proved we were meant to play a significant part in each other's lives. But it was not to be. Egypt's revolution came to symbolise our relationship. Strength and sincerity were discarded, and shattered fragments of truth are the remnants.

It lasted four months and ten days. He loved me, but his mother refused to accept me. She gave him an ultimatum – to choose me or his family. I didn't want him to have to make that choice, but I did expect more from him, a valiant effort to convince. But he said he was torn, that he had no choice. He lost hope, weighted by his certainty that she wouldn't change her mind.

We remained close for months after, until his behaviour revealed flaws, weakness of character, belying the man I thought he was. Distrust and hypocrisy dissolved the compounds of love, leaving behind a dull precipitate from damaged hearts.

But what started with a *duah*, and ended with smiles and eventually tears, remains a symbol of faith. I trust in Allah's Will. I live by one mantra, *Allahu Aalam* – "Allah knows best". I've forgiven him and bear no animosity toward him or his parents. Paralysed pain was a magnet drawing me to my *musallah*, twilight tears were seekers of *tahajjud*. Every time I questioned, every time I felt despair, I turned to the One True Comforter. My ego shattered, I found contentment in faith. It is this certainty of faith, this belief in *taqdeer*, which allows me to feel comfortable being single. If not for this, my *nafs* would be wallowing in envy, my mind rotting in insecurity, my heart mourning in self-induced grief, and my soul would be dead. In the past year, all my previously unattached South African friends have married or become engaged. I was asked if this makes me despondent. On the contrary, it fills me with a lightness of being, happiness for them, which translates into hope for me.

I left Egypt in July 2011, following months of introspection and indecision. It was *istikhara* which guided me back home to South Africa. I sacrificed a burgeoning career as a foreign correspondent, willingly forsaking transience for the prospect of permanence. I told myself the next overseas country I would live in would be with my husband.

But my resolve wavers. As days unfurl in a drought devoid of serendipitous meetings which hold promise, my career is showered by fellowships, awards and job opportunities. Ah, the irony of fate. Allah Knows Best. Perhaps it is in my *naseeb* to find a partner through the pursuit of a career, not in the abandonment of it.

I no longer have a timeline dictating to me supposed milestones, as determined by myself, family and society. As I wait to meet a man who is as worthy of me as I am of him, I will continue to live a fulfilled life in this limbo of longing to be a wife and mother.

And when the desert winds of my spirit howl in lonely yearning, I will find peace in prayer, the only absolute constant.

PART TWO

Identity

Surrounded by women of strength

Rehana Moosajee

Sitting on Seat 5B, business class of Delta Airlines, flying from Seattle to Atlanta and then transferring on to Johannesburg – the girl from Lenasia – is it possible? "I have just been the keynote speaker at the American Association of Public Transport – 1 500 experts on transport in the USA who were intrigued, enthralled and inspired by a South African woman from Johannesburg – is this out of a movie or am I simply dreaming?"

My mother's words resonate in my ears, "You are studying but you know the family you want to marry into don't want women to work. Won't it all be a waste?" I remember being adamant that it could do no harm to secure a degree even if in all likelihood I would end up cooking *biryani*, filling *samoosas* and being a dutiful wife, mother, daughter and daughter in-law. It was unlikely that in those teenage years I could have envisaged that life is not something we plan, have control over or design by ourselves.

By age twenty-two, I was divorced and by twenty-four, married to Salim, the man who continues to encourage me to be everything I want to be, to discover myself, the world, to mother our two teenage children in unconventional ways, to explore both my spirituality and my sensuality and to get the most out of life.

For so much of my life, I had depended on the approval of others. I tried to fit in, conform, be the good Muslim girl of Indian descent, who lives according to the script. Go to school, get an education, get married, have kids. If you work – you will still do everything that stay-at-home wives and mothers do and when your children are grown, especially your daughters, repeat the cycle. Life chose not to deal me the conventional deck of cards and I chose not to let up on the opportunities to do more, be more – staying true to my favourite movie line of all time, "Carpe Diem: Seize the Day", as espoused in *Dead Poet's Society*.

As I reflect, I realise it's because I have been blessed to be surrounded by people of character – women of strength and strong men who were not threatened by allowing the women in their lives to shine.

My *Dadima* – ninety-one years old and still enjoying life – had the insight and foresight to encourage my mother, her daughter-in-law, to pursue her teaching career, rather than settle in Ottosdal, a small *dorpie* in the Western Transvaal. She encouraged my father to go to Johannesburg and start his life with his new bride and later family. She worked tirelessly at my grandfather's side, rising early to roast peanuts and fry fish to sell in the cafe. *Dadima* has always been a strong-headed, fiercely independent woman, who would sometimes have four o' clock tea, made for her, by *Bajee*, a most gentle man. He understood her and accepted her and they would do gardening together, argue and bicker, chat and laugh – most of all enjoying the times when family were around them. *Dadima*, after *Bajee* passed away, did a most unconventional thing; she followed her heart and went to stay with her daughter, even though she has three sons, who would gladly have welcomed her into their homes. Her sons, secure in themselves, have never felt affronted by this and the love and care between them is palpable. *Dadima*, even at age ninety-one, enjoys my outrageous birthday parties and merrily goes along with my crazy ideas, and enjoys the parties we throw for her even more!

Then there's "*Ophirton Ma*" or *Nanima* – my maternal grandmother, married to the other *Bajee*, who was much sterner. My *Nanima* was brave and courageous – giving life to eight daughters and six sons, making a plan for putting food on the table, when the family business was ailing because *Bajee* was either too philosophical or too trusting. She just got on with the practicality of raising family, with an entrepreneurial spirit that saw her selling plates of food to the mineworkers or barring the doors of the shop when riots were imminent. She apparently had single handedly killed a snake in Zeerust. She bore steadfastly and with resolve the roller coaster that is life: liquidation of the family business, 14 pregnancies and a husband who chose after that to take a second wife, the onset of diabetes and the waxing and waning of the fortunes of her offspring and grandchildren. *Nanima's* younger daughters were encouraged to pursue education and careers: two became teachers and one a doctor, in an era when most girls felt that getting married and living happily ever after was the recipe for life.

My mother was one of the daughters who pursued teaching. Having met my father at a relatively young age, she got her teaching qualification after Standard Eight and then got married. So, when I was in Grade One and Two my mother was studying to complete her Matric. When I was in Standard Nine and Matric, my mother was furthering her studies, enrolled as a full time student at Laudium College, traveling daily from Lenasia and still fulfilling all the home front responsibilities. Over the years, my father encouraged my mother. She was promoted from a Level One educator to Head of Department and finally the principal of Bree Primary School – the same school where she had been a pupil and started her career. Over the years, she has imparted the gift of reading and writing to thousands of children, many of whom still come to greet her in a mall – now raising children of their own. She grew to love cricket, my father's passion. She and her sister have traveled extensively, exploring foreign cultures and cities, meeting new people. Whilst doing all this she has been a pillar of strength to the extended family and friends in times of joy and heartache.

And then of course there are the numerous women, teachers, aunts, cousins, spiritual mentors, friends, domestic helpers, colleagues, comrades, and in-laws, all of whom have encouraged me to do more and be more. They have scolded, criticised, helped, supported, understood, beheld or just been present. I realise that Allah has truly blessed me with the people, opportunities and experiences that have enriched my life. In my 43 years on this earth I have been blessed to experience love, birth, death, success, failure, excruciating pain, heartfelt joy and inner peace. I know that life's chapters can't be written by me, that all I can do is behold it all with immense gratitude and as I reflect, know that we all can affect our own lives by the attitude when we choose to respond to the things that happen to us.

I remember defining moments: a camp at St Stithians school in 1984, EduTrain in 1993, my first trip to London on my own in 1993, Peace of Mind Retreat in Rajastan in 2005, Dadi Janki's 90th birthday in Oxford in 2006, an inter faith and inter cultural trip to Turkey in 2007. Meeting people from Soweto and Stockholm, speaking in Brussels and Bonn, making friends in Bogota and Boksburg, from

Madrid to *masjids* in Midrand. The Voice Radio station raising the voice of the voiceless. Contesting elections and losing, the pastor who prayed for me in a Church, the Guru who blessed me in a temple and the criticism received when I dared to pray *Eid salaah* with my one-year-old son in my arms. From spectacular sunrises to glorious sunsets, from outrageous birthday parties to the loss of loved ones. There have been trials and tribulations but equally there has been joy and jubilation. I have no idea when it will end, but it seems opportune to remember the lyrics of a song I so liked, "I am what I am and what I am needs no excuses. I beat my own drum – some think its noise, I think it's pretty …"

So, as this Delta flight approaches Atlanta airport, I realise that my life thus far is really as a result of the amazingly strong women whose examples have impacted me in such profound ways. As I think of my 16-year-old daughter Faheemah, in Istanbul on her first international trip, I pray she will be surrounded by women of strength and men who are strong enough to embrace it!

The creation of complex me

Nabeelah Patel

My name is Nabeelah Patel. So what's there to say? Here I am, trying to describe my bleak existence to bring some sort of understanding as to who I truly am, if that's possible. I often question my existence and in doing so I'm boggled by many thoughts and theories. As human beings we are not programmed to follow one specific code, or … are we? Some scholars argue that our paths have already been drawn and we are merely pawns on a chess board. I believe that it is our differences and experiences that make us who we are and define us as individuals even though we still are members of a group, a community. I would like to think I am different to the community I reside in. Do I belong to it? Well … I don't really know … I guess that these questions all contribute to the design, the creation of complex me.

My life started when my dad left. At the age of eight, I moved out of my perfect little white picket-fenced house in the suburbs. My ideal world was left behind to join the cold real world. There is not much I can say about my father. I don't know him very well and haven't had many years of his company. There was a time where I would wonder where he was or how he was. Now … I don't care. I have my own life and interests that my father is not a part of. He does not know me and did not take the time to get to know me. In my teen years this would bother me extensively and I would try to stay in touch with him but to no avail. I often wonder about him not wanting me around but I try not to think about him anymore. I'm angry now and if he had to turn up one day, I'd probably just chase him away. So even though we don't live in a picket-fenced house anymore, I know that I am truly loved by the family that shares my home – my mother, my brother and my sister-in-law, Sa'diyya.

Moving out was moving on and it was not the first of many unfortunate events. That's the thing about life. Sometimes you have just got to pick up the pieces and move forward because you don't know how bright the future might be.

I attribute the bulk of my success to my mother. Without all the years of her love and devotion I would not be where I am today. My inner strength and ability to propel my energy into a positive sphere comes from living out the example my mother has set for me. All the years of love, laughter, tears and passed-down wisdom has made me the contented person I am today. As each day passes, I see more of my mother in me and nothing in this world pleases me more.

My mother has also afforded me the opportunity to meet some of the great people in this country. From Deputy President Kgalema Motlanthe and the great Ahmed Kathrada to the late Kader Asmal, I have been blessed to have been in their presence. This is not only good for my own self improvement but for my career as well. Someday I will be one of the greats. Someday my name will be in lights for having made this world a better place.

Life wasn't always so rosy though. There was a time when my family and I had to make sacrifices. My mum took to doing catering to make ends meet for my brother and me. Even in our darkest hour, I can never remember being short of anything. Things soon took a turn for the better when I was nearing the end of my schooling and my mum got a job as the Mayor's personal assistant.

But in order to reach the light one must journey into a tunnel of darkness. The bane of my childhood was my years spent at the "Islamic" School. This place was filled with the fairest skinned people in the whitest of robes who had the blackest of characters – that's my opinion anyway … The vast wealth division further isolated me as I did not meet their standards of attractiveness nor affluence. Your status in school was not based on merit, but rather on your parent's bank balance. Over and above the scorn faced from both teachers and learners alike, I was also at the forefront of being falsely accused of stealing and cheating. My resentment of this place and its inhabitants cannot be ignored.

All that life throws at you, good or bad, is a lesson and a test. What is important is to absorb the positive and discredit the negative. I learnt to respect all people for who they are and not the colour of their skin or their bank balance or their popularity. Fortunately, I completed my schooling at a different school and since then my life has been blessed in many ways.

The apex of my life thus far would have to be my university

years. I put my heart and soul into academia. I fell in love with the greats, such as, Shakespeare, Hemingway, Wilde and Yeats. Ensuring that I excelled in the academic field was most satisfactory as it was like giving every critic a huge slap across their face. Adjusting to an academic surrounding, studying literature and meeting interesting people outside my red-neck home town was amazing. At university there is no constant preaching of religious dogma and everything you do, and the choices you make, aren't scrutinised under a microscope of judgement.

At university I met my best friend Maria – a blonde Greek girl, who taught me to always be myself. She would always say, "this is you in all of your splendour and it doesn't get any better than this". Despite us being in different faculties at university, we are still the best of friends and chat about everything from fashion and food to work and men. Having had night-long conversations with Maria, who has a totally different heritage to mine, I have learnt that irrespective of colour, creed, culture or era, women are expected to fulfill the same cultural obligations and expectations. These include marrying and producing offspring by a certain age. I do not see myself as being fit, nor ready, for this sort of commitment.

There is someone that tickles my fancy though. His name is Jimmy. He is tall, with a clean-shaven head and beard and always wears a black Rip Curl cap. Our personalities are very much in sync, but the primary attraction to Jimmy would have to be his intellect. My biggest weakness in men would have to be intelligence. I love the fact that he reads good books and watches good movies. Also, his ability to absorb the deeper messages in literature and film is another positive factor.

I would probably be discouraged from pursuing him as a love interest. Many would say he is not suited to a Muslim lifestyle. I often question this religious expectation mainly because my father is Muslim and yet he left us as young children in the care of only my mother. I often wonder about his religious beliefs and his expectations of being a father to us. Do you walk out without looking back solely because you, somewhere on your life's journey, realised that the woman you married is not the one for you? Being intimate with somebody is difficult; we are not animals who consummate for the sole purpose of breeding. Surely being Muslim like my father is, gives you the conscience to realise that after having two children with a woman you once loved, you cannot just walk away.

I find my comfort with Jimmy, perhaps because for now he appears to be so different from my father. He is a psychology student and through our conversations, he helps me understand myself better. He may not be the perfect man for a Muslim woman, but sometimes I think he is the perfect person for me. Friend, boyfriend or partner: anyone who can quote Oscar Wilde, know every character in Spiderman and has read "Fight Club" is a mate worth having, in my book.

Pressures to get married are always there. However these pressures come with conditions attached. He must be from the same village in India that you both haven't heard of and he must be a Muslim. Jimmy is neither of these things. Most people would look at this and believe that it is "doomed to fail". For the most obvious reasons they would be right. Although, loving someone, or even really liking them, can blind you into not seeing those reasons so clearly. It becomes hard to choose between what you want and what is right.

What defines me as a person would have to be my education. I love to learn about and explore many different cultures, art, cinema, literature and theatre. My bottom line philosophy would have to be that whether you are watching a masterpiece like *The Godfather* or frivolous television shows like *Gossip Girl*, there is always something to learn. I am not the smartest human being on earth and each friend I choose to have is an asset in my life, someone I can learn from and relate to. You can never know too much and even the wisest of men always has something to learn. I choose to live my life without believing that I am better than the next person, which was the mentality of many people I was exposed to in my early years. Spending my life living in a little red-neck Indian town has put me off the small town mentality and ways of living. Being best friends with a Greek girl and interested in a non-Muslim man would probably suggest how far away I prefer to be from the people that haunt my past.

Becoming a professional, finding Mr Right, travelling and being on a path of self discovery is a taxing task. It is even more taxing when you have to subscribe to religious and cultural practices. Don't get me wrong, I am not here to blashpheme upon you. In my life as it stands, there are endless pressures and high expectations, ones that I am not even sure I can fulfill. Having too much to deal with can be a form of entrapment. Here, you must choose which direction is best for you.

I won't hate those that want to be stay-at-home wives and settle down at a young age. I just don't see myself marching to that drum beat. After I complete my Master's Degree, I would like to travel. Being an International Relations student, the urge to visit the countries and regions I have studied grows larger each year. East Asia, Europe and Latin America would be my favourite destinations.

The way I see life right now is that there is so much to it. For me, marriage would be a constraint. I couldn't possibly wear those invisible handcuffs and put all my dreams on hold for commitment. I would very much like to meet Mr Right. I know that I have no control over when that will happen – I am just not ready for it to happen right now. First, I need to blossom into a flower from a bud and settle into my own life. In this big, bad world I don't know where I'll end up, or who I will be, but I need to find that out first. I need to fathom the complex me, settle into my skin and breathe …

About ME

Salma Mangera

An amazing soul, whose life is and always will be inextricably linked to mine, once offered me this epiphany, "I like living my life in neat little boxes." I heard this after I had survived my tempestuous teens and was well into my adult years. Labels, definitions, constraints, judgments, forced morality – existential crisis!

Forced into confronting my "ME"-ness, I am faced with searching for a linear definition to best describe me. Who am I? Muslim, Indian, Female Speech Therapist? Female Muslim Indian Speech Therapist? All powerful, ever incredible, aspirational, inspirational Woman?

I am "fabulously forty", somewhere between "*laat lammetjies*" and menopause and can honestly claim to finally be happy in my skin. It has been a challenging and rewarding journey, as life promises to be, and I feel blessed. So many things fashion how I forge ahead in this crazy, beautiful world and I continue in the unending evolution of my spiritual growth.

By definition, I would classify myself as unconventional. I bear this mantle with pride and refuse to conform to any but my own divinely guided beliefs. Apartheid curbed possibilities, something unknown to the youth of today. I matriculated in the eighties under the "prestigious" department of "Indian" education. Unlimited "A"s was virtually impossible. I applied to the much lauded University of the Witwatersrand for the opportunity to study within the field of Speech Therapy and Audiology. Obviously my humble credentials proved less than satisfactory because I was offered along with nine other non-white people a tepid substitution in the form of an ill – conceived, token diploma, in Community Speech and Hearing Therapy – an auxiliary qualification to satisfy the illusion of accommodating "everyone" within the Wits autocracy. It was almost as if those of us of darker hues needed to prove that we would be relatively on par with our fairer counterparts. My paternal grandfather impressed on me that a journey does not always need to be travelled in one straight, uninterrupted way, so I qualified six years later having cruised through the two year diploma and my Honours degree in Speech Therapy and Audiology. Contrary to popular belief, all females enrolled for an arts degree do not automatically find engineer, accountant or doctor husbands before the end of their course. Unless, according to the Muslim-daughter-in-law barometer, I was simply not "fair enough" and made lousy tea to boot.

My mother and I enjoyed a super volatile relationship as I was growing up as we were both assertive, strong willed, opinionated women. Me, in training, and her, married young and into the most esteemed of all careers, professional motherhood. My mini-skirted, wild haired, rebellious self was a stark contrast to her Muslim mummy values, but I was of her, regardless. She threatened me millions of times that I would reap my just dues when my daughter was born, but I was all too sure that was never to be, as I hurried past my traditional Muslim women marriage sell-by-date. My first love resurfaced as a phoenix, to make me the unique offer of being wife number two. Polygamy is totally acceptable in Islam, my religion, but unpalatable to my modern Muslim identity. I remain eternally grateful to my younger brother for playing the game according to the rules and marrying young, so that my parents' needs were more than promptly and adequately realised as they became "in-laws" to my brother's wife and grandparents to their children. Members of my loving extended family and close-knit community wondered if my education had rendered me "too clever" to be a wife for most.

My work as a speech therapist at a school for learners with severe intellectual challenges for the past twenty years is less about what I do than who I am. About thirteen years ago, after playfully imploring the female principal of an almost totally female staff complement to do me a huge favour by employing the rarest of all life forms, a handsome male educator in South African education, I found on my return from *Hajj* in 2000 that my soul mate had arrived. My prayers had been answered. The ultimate spiritual homecoming! I arrived *burkah* free but cloaked in newfound spirituality and acceptance.

Miles away from fenced in convention, my beautiful "black" husband -to-be embraced my religion. Pieces of a perfectly predestined interlocking puzzle, *Alhamdullilah*, a perfect fit. My family was enchanted and I concerned myself with only the judgments of those who mattered. The overt hypocrisy of those who valued an incredible being only because he chose to follow their faith initially stung. I was offended to no end by the happy back clappers who told me that I would be rewarded in the hereafter for bringing one to the fold, when my heaven is here and now.

My mother's prophecy held true, and my miraculous daughter is mini-me magnified. As a family, we have acclimatised to the not-so-subtle ping pong matches which play out when we're out in public together. We celebrate that this is ours, as a few years ago, it could not legally have been.

A day before my daughter's fourth birthday, my mother was unceremoniously plucked from our lives after performing the late afternoon prayers with her aged and ailing mother. The loss of one's mother almost single-handedly re-defines one's being. An inevitable chasm opened, so vast that I know it will render me somewhat incomplete until we meet again.

In terms of my purpose in this world, I believe that Allah bestows a gift specific to each and every one of us, and we are obliged by His grace to share it The fundamental goal is to love, be loved and to make a difference. Too often we get seduced by accumulating things along the way; wealth, acclaim, pleasure, fame, finding that we need to retrace every once in awhile to do what is real. For instance, we practice contrived, well intentioned, orchestrated acts of charity and largesse like sixty seven minutes in honour of Nelson Mandela rather than emulating his pristine way of life every living moment.

Words are my weapon of choice and my panacea too. I have always been heard, as the first grandchild, as one who can talk the talk, as a confident, assertive communicator, as the "entertainment centre" as my mother would call me, and as a professional. It is the reason that the focus of my life's work is providing a voice to the most marginalised of all people, children with disabilities. You know that your purpose is being fulfilled when appraisal arrives in the form of prayers from parents and when inclusion is a matter of principle, and not dictates; when we acknowledge that we are in essence souls in unison celebrating our diversity rather than clamouring for the moral high ground; when the superpowers are those who channel positive energy, rather than the fiscal nuclei of a finite universe; when we cease to be colours, numbers, or gender specific prototypes; when the haves and the have-nots merge into one instead of being polar extremes on an endless continuum; when religion is sacred, whether it is yours, mine, ours, theirs or indefinable. When we can live and let live. Say and do as you must in this lifetime rather than have eulogy related upon one's passing. The truest reflection of God in your life is integrity, respect and unconditional positive regard. It's not always about me, but I will be heard.

Reflections

Yasmin Denat

He's gone again … he left this morning, I hate when he leaves. The muffled goodbyes, the stifled tears, and the promise of divine protection – it never seems to get any easier. Actually, with three kids under the age of eight it's getting much more demanding. But now, I understand. Alas, this is the way my life is and now I would have it no other way! It's never been about fear of calamity or loneliness. On the contrary it has always been about need, me needing him. As pathetic as that may sound coming from a 21st century woman – it's true! But his love for me has positively altered me. He has made me realise that we have to make our bond about something greater, to find the essence of eternal love.

To say the least, the last decade has been a complete metamorphosis. Whether I emerge as the ever mystical, bright winged, fluttering butterfly remains to be seen. Perhaps there will emerge a wide eyed warty toad on the other end of this meandering tale … but then again this is not a tale – it does not begin with "once upon a time" and there are no heroes or love woes. This is merely a reflection of a state of mind and a condition of the soul. It is as fragmented as the reflection of a mosaic.

You see, my other half, my soul mate – he has a dream, and as selfish as it may appear to the majority of the world – his dream does not include me. He seeks to conquer the world, nay, not with the sword, nor with success – but with the word of Allah. His mission, as is the mission of millions of others, is noble to some, wildly selfish and naive to others. Needless to say the work of the *tablighi's,* as they have become known, is widely discussed and debated, loved and hated. So here I am, "the *tablighi's* wife".

It is the first of my 40 days. I wake up as usual at 6:15 but the stillness in the air is different when he has not slept beside me. It is the final time for *Fajr*, so I will have to get up quickly. I climb stealthily out, hoping that my six-month-old will not stir. I pass the full length bedroom mirror in the muted morning light and catch a glimpse of my silhouette. I attempt to see myself from the outside, I can scarcely believe my age. I often still pass as a "young mother" but I have also become an "aunty". Yes, it has to be acknowledged – I don't pass as "cool" anymore! But aesthetics are no longer the centre of my life. I look after myself: take pride in what I wear, but it is definitely not as significant as it once was. I try to make the external reflect the internal.

My love for my husband began in the worst fashion – in the halls of academia against all Islamic principles. It is a constant noose around my neck, I beg for divine pardon. But miraculously in the end I have been given the blessing of fulfillment and joy. He has opened my soul to the purpose of my living, to be a better Muslim. He has made Islam my life. The attraction of tertiary institutions and corporate glory has faded. Now I am truly me.

I would have probably died of shame, embarrassment and sheer distress if someone ten years ago had said that in my early thirties I would be rearing three kids and have no vocation, indeed as loath as I may be to say it – I have been domesticated! Yikes! I have swapped the boardroom for the kitchen and literary greats for random mass market novels.

For a mother of three, leisure time is rare and precious, but during those much treasured moments of stillness – I still ponder. But the direction of my pondering has most definitely taken a new course. I no longer ponder the meaning of life, the purpose of my individual being or the manner by which I shall achieve my lifelong goals … no, I have not aged and my love for life has not diminished. It is merely that I have been redirected and have been blessed with a greater spiritual sense of the world.

As a parent myself I now look at my parents in a different light. I recognise life's cyclical bond of parent and child, for with each child a new hope is born. Each time I have been given my newborn to hold for the first time I am always in awe, in absolute reverence and gratitude. When I look into my mother's eyes as they light up when she sees my children, I see her love for me. When the veins on my father's forehead pulsate as he sits beside me in hospital next to my sick child, I see his pain and I know he hurts for me …

It's all about redefining expectations; I have changed the lenses with which I see the world. As is the case with all change, the exact moment of change can never be precisely identified, so the exact moment that I was transformed from a pen-wielding poetry-quoting academic into a pot-stirring, nappy-changing, sleep-deprived, car-pooling *hijab*-clad mom – will forever remain a mystery. Yes, somewhere along my trip I moved from Descartes to diapers! But truth be told it seemed like a natural enough process, save for a few moments of utter frustration, but these were quickly erased by an eager toddler's sloppy kisses.

My love, as I have said, has been redefined for me. My romantic love no longer lies in candle-lit dinners but in late-night whispered conversations over the heads of three sleeping children. My love for my parents, spouse, children, sister and all who inhabit my small world is now selfless, governed by a greater law, the all-encompassing law of divinity. Even though when I sit on my *musallah* five times a day I am never in the zone of complete devotion that I seek, I acknowledge that this is my purpose and it is this knowledge alone that has given me completeness, sanctity and peace.

Just the other day I was at the airport, standing with loved ones at International Departures, without luggage mind you, because yet again it was not me who was going on a grand trip, not me who was going on business, not me who was going on pilgrimage. No, I was just there to say "bye", to wish them well; but that's ok, because I will be the one at home telling elaborate tales of exotic lands to the eager eyes, ears and bodies that drape themselves on the floor beside me. So in the past I may have felt as if I had never truly "arrived", I now enjoy sending others off to international destinations of great grandeur. Because on some deeper level, I now understand that this is my journey, and I will live completely in the here and now to enjoy what is, instead of wondering what could have been … This is the choice I have made and I choose to live my life without regret. It is not a matter of self-aggrandizement, rather it is treading the path of love.

So now when I am left alone at home on an annual basis for the spiritual benefit of humanity, I no longer see it as sacrificial. It is about growth, personal growth. In writing I'm attempting to grow, to make my dream of becoming a writer a reality. During the course of my postgraduate degree, I was told that editors were failed writers. In the end I would have even settled for that. This is how profound my love for the written word is.

I once read that an average four-year-old asks in the region of 460 questions in the course of a single day. I do not find this at all shocking, because that's what I do all day; I answer more questions than a university lecturer on average. I have to be more creative than a movie director and I analyse the actions of my kids with more depth than a psychoanalyst. So I have never remained under-stimulated in any way. I have just always felt inclined to write. A combination of lack of creative imagination and lack of literary genius has always harnessed my ambitions.

But I am no longer going through identity crises, I have embraced who I am. I am a Muslim mother, sister, wife and daughter. I know now that the world is not as I once thought it to be. Even though I have not climbed Everest or written the most earth-shattering novel of the 21st century, I have found my greatness.

In the last eight years I have been given inspiration from a daughter with an all-encompassing spirit who has succeeded against all odds, intelligence in another daughter whose independence and zeal leaves me speechless, and prosperity in a son who has demonstrated that love is true wealth. So when I leave to drop my kids at school I pause to throw on my *abaya* and *hijab* and the only truth I am sure of, is that I am happy that I am not as I once was, even though I am not exactly as I wish to be …

Only "Oomi!"

Zaheera Jina

It's my sixth year of doing a PhD. The realisation makes me falter. My vision is suddenly blurry and tears spill from my eyes. I'm caught. I trudge along in eager anticipation of completing and then, just like a slimy snail on a wall, I slide many spaces down. They say that this is the hero's journey; I ask, at what expense?

It's two in the morning again. I have been rotating inside this time capsule for many days now. I work through the early hours of the morning, till dawn breaks. I then dress in "*Oomi* attire" and entertain my toddler till his midday sleep. I need to. I owe it to him. My younger brother believes that the government should implement interviews for couples before they consider having children. He argues that mothers must be responsible for nurturing their young and if they cannot, they should choose not to get pregnant. Simple. Or is it?

I have always chosen that "*Oomi* thing". I chose to be the *Oomi* when we played "house" as kids. I imitated carrying a doll on my hips the way my mother carried my younger brother when he was a baby. I wanted to be married and I wanted to be "mommy" or *Oomi* to many little offspring. My dream, from the ripe age of twenty-one, was to be a good, pretty wife to a man who would care for me, love and cherish me and of course I, him.

I didn't anticipate waiting a decade. The "aunties" brought every Mr Eligible home to "see" me; the final count was somewhere between thirty-five and forty-eight visits. My weekends were spent baking, entertaining, or filling *samoosas* for the next date that had been set. The response was always the same: "*bou oonchie*!" The "aunties" warned my family suspiciously that the evil eye was on me. They related stories of beautiful, fair maidens who never married because they were struck by *nazar* or, worse still, *jadoo*! And so I was shuttled off to the *Moulana* for his diagnosis and returned home with *taweez* and incense to burn and prayers to read. I am religious and I believed that Allah had a plan, but I still yearned for the love so beautifully described in romance novels. A friend advised that the path to finding Mr Right was similar to catching a butterfly. You can eagerly try to catch the butterfly without success, then, when you least expect it, it will settle on your shoulder.

Suleiman came into my life at a point in time when Allah, in his infinite wisdom, thought it was the best time possible. My parents were happy and so was I, and I am thankful to my *Creator* because Suleiman and I are compatible in our Islamic values and beliefs. By then, I had entered my journey into academia and had given up on the idea of marrying. I had completed my master's degree at Wits University and, at my supervisor's suggestion, I had adopted a PhD baby: a baby who kept me up through nights of intellectual thought and days of unanswered questions; who I carried around swaddled in my brain; and who came with me into my marriage with Suleiman. And now I have two babies and both of them are demanding and expect my full concentration.

For the first two years of Yusuf's life and in the analysis stages of my PhD journey, I lived a roller coaster ride, trying to juggle the trials of first-time motherhood and the emotional upheavals brought about by my own mother's cancer diagnosis. My PhD stagnated. But there are rainbows after thunderstorms, and it went well for a while after that. Yusuf, my toddler, was accommodating of my studies. He was too young to know any better. I went to university for a few hours on certain days and left him with my mother-in-law, feeling confident that he would be well taken care of. He was doing fine and was learning to be independent.

It all changed the day I returned home a bit later than expected. My son had become ill. I blame myself. Yusuf now hates it when I work at my computer; an unnatural jealousy has grown between my toddler and my PhD baby. I have often contemplated giving up the PhD. Suleiman urges that I don't. Anyway, there is far too much bursary funding to pay back, if I do. I have gotten so far and yet at this point I'm sliding down, like that snail on the wall.

Everywhere we go, people ask when we are planning baby number two. (Baby number two or three?) My supervisor has advised me to wait until I have seen my PhD baby to completion. Fellow academics have warned the same; they say that growing yet another baby would be too demanding and I would never graduate.

I want to have another baby and we are actively trying. Yusuf needs a sibling and the clock ticks on. I have a silent battle raging within me: I calculate and plan towards ovulation dates and, when that time of the month draws closer, I wait anxiously with hope and fear. I experience symptoms of nausea and I believe that I am pregnant but, with the arrival of "Aunty Rosie", I'm left empty and forlorn like a dark, deserted tunnel. It's a feeling of incompleteness and, as I grow older, age chases me like an old woman with a *champal* – making it more difficult with each increasing slash. The fertility specialist asked if I am generally a stressed human being.

Am I stressed? Should I be stressed?

My eyes feel heavy and the words on the screen start rotating. I yearn to go and lie with my husband and toddler while they sleep but I remind myself that I cannot do any PhD writing in the hours that Yusuf is awake. So, as I stare at my PhD baby in a desperate attempt to make some conceptual sense of it, my toddler sleeps on and, when he awakens, I will rush to his call – shutting down my computer, throwing out the many empty wrappers of chocolates. I sigh … I am exhausted. I don't want to be the hero on my journey; I want to be only "*Oomi*".

Domination versus submission

Anonymous

Even as I write this, I feel that all too familiar uneasiness rising up from my tummy. My story is one of two extremes: the ultimate career woman, and the devoted traditional woman. These extremes are easily married by most women, but continue to be a source of conflict for me. I read an interesting post on a Facebook page today where a man theorised that the struggle between balancing career and home for women of the 21st century lies in a very simple dilemma … Domination versus Submission.

In High School, I was the "A student". I matriculated fourth in my school and my name still holds pride of place on my school's board of highest achievers. When I was young, I dreamt of being a successful career woman. I wanted to hold a high position and earn my own money. I wanted to be the independent, strong woman I saw on all those television shows I watched. I also dreamt of being happily married and having children to whom I would devote my time. It was with this vision of my future, and the fact that I come from a home of medical professionals, that I decided to apply to study either Physiotherapy or Speech Therapy at university. Physiotherapy was my first choice, but unfortunately I was only accepted for Speech Therapy. In hindsight I think that this story would read very differently if I had studied Physiotherapy instead of Speech Therapy, but Speech Therapy was in my *taqdeer* and I embraced that choice whole heartedly.

Like most young, impressionable girls, I went off to university and fell head over heels in love with almost the first guy I met. He is now my husband and the love of my life. Something weird happened when I met him and when we became close. All of a sudden, I felt the pull of tradition. This man was not a dominating traditional man by a long shot, he loved the fact that I was intelligent and pursuing a career. He loved the fact that we could challenge each other intellectually and that occasionally, I could even correct his medical knowledge. When we spoke of the future, it always included my career alongside his, like a partnership. I also made it clear to him that I intended to contribute to all the household expenses as much as he did. I did not want to be a "kept woman" or worse yet, a "housewife". Yet after a while, all I wanted to do was just get married, have babies and stay home to cook and clean. It was mind-boggling!

Eventually, I graduated as a Speech Therapist and Audiologist. As much as I had tried to develop a deep love and passion for my profession, it was never as consuming as for some of my peers who lived and breathed Speech Therapy and Audiology. I went on to do my community service, for which I was placed in a rural community clinic structure with not much in the way of resources. It was definitely a learning curve. I loved earning a salary for the first time in my life. I was living that life that I dreamt of in school. I had my own car which I had paid for, I was living on my own and paying my own rent. I was "powerful" and in control … but I was also lonely …

It was a tough year in which my family experienced a lot of stress and trauma. My brother fell gravely ill and we didn't know if he was going to survive. *Alhamdulillah* through the power of *duah*, he made a complete recovery. Soon after his recovery, my sister contracted meningitis and had to be hospitalised – yet another traumatic experience, but *Subhanallah* it was very mild and she recovered completely and quickly. Just when we thought it wouldn't get worse, all the stress seemed to take its toll on my father who developed severe blockages in at least three of his heart blood vessels, requiring him to undergo a triple heart bypass.

Needless to say, all of those incidents had an everlasting impact on me and my entire family. I began to reflect on life and what is most important. What I realised was that money comes and goes and no matter how much time you spend at work, your colleagues will never be your family. I realised that my faith in my Allah and my family was what was most important. I often think it was those traumatic moments when my dearest loved ones were ill that became the catalyst for the life that I now lead.

I got engaged at the end of my community service year, a ray of light that shone through the darkness. My wedding was four months later. It was a beautiful occasion. The uniting of two souls and two families for the pleasure of Allah and a moment I had looked forward to my whole life. Between my engagement and wedding, I did not work. I focused on planning my wedding. I loved the time that I did not work. Perhaps I loved it too much. I recall a conversation I had with a friend a few weeks before my wedding. She asked me if I intended on getting back to work immediately after the honeymoon (of course it was assumed that I would work at some point since that is the norm these days). I remember hesitating for a long while before replying that I guessed I would start applying for jobs after I'd settled in at my new home. Sensing my hesitation, she asked if we were planning on starting a family anytime soon. If she had asked that question the previous year, I would have immediately replied with a firm "No!" but instead I truthfully told her, "Whatever Allah wills. I've worked, I've lived alone, I've been independent, I've experienced most of what I've wanted to. I'm not getting any younger so if it is willed for me to have a baby soon then *Alhamdulillah* I will be delighted." My friend promptly replied with, "Yoh! Who are you and what have you done with my friend?!" It was very funny at the time, but these were the early signs that a revolution was brewing inside me.

The wedding was in April, we honeymooned until early May. About a month after the wedding, my husband and I spoke about the future in terms of me working or not. My husband being the gracious person that he is, told me that it was my choice whether I wanted to work or not. He will not tell me not to or force me to either. It was my choice. I was relieved that he didn't expect me to work. I felt free which was an odd feeling to feel since I was supposed to be a "new age woman". I decided I would give myself time to just be a wife. I would focus on building a strong foundation for my marriage and explore the homely side of myself since it beckoned so strongly. I thought I would get bored after a few months and that I would run back into the working world without looking back for one second. What I didn't expect was that I would love it. That I would feel as if I was living my best life, that I had finally found a purpose. Being a "housewife"! How strange …

In the beginning, when people asked me when I intended to go back to work, I would confidently respond with the truth that I was enjoying being a housewife and just exploring this phase until work beckoned. After six months though, I realised that I may never get the urge to go back to work. At that point the questions I received were less about making small talk and more expressing genuine concern that I was throwing my entire education and essentially my life away by sitting at home like the "kept" women I once thought of as being pathetic. My mother, who was also educated but was forced by my father to become a housewife, once told me quite sternly that I had studied for so long and worked so hard for the education I received that I should not throw it all away, and also that I should help my husband out with the costs of running a household in these trying times. She had a point and I felt horrible and useless and sort of like I was taking up space instead of contributing to society in any way. I agonised over this constantly. Every day I would sit in front of the computer looking for jobs and attempting to get my CV together so as to start applying. However the thought of going back to work made me feel sick. I was not excited at the prospect at all. There were no jobs available at that time which comforted me oddly and that became my new answer when I would get asked about my return to work. My husband sensed that I was at conflict about these decisions and he reminded me that we were managing financially so I could do as I pleased. May Allah bless him for being so kind and understanding. His kindness and reassurance made me realise something else, that if I returned to work it was more about the money and contributing to the household in the way that I had envisioned, instead of it being out of a love for the type of work I would be doing or just to immerse myself in my profession again. It was at that point that I realised that I would probably never return to work unless there was a financial need for me to.

It sounded selfish, I'm a therapist and therefore I should have a need to work other than for money, I could be out there helping others but … I felt nothing. My mind was plagued by many questions … Has my husband secretly lost respect for me because I'm not the career driven woman I was when we first met? Am I not living up to my potential? Am I letting myself down? Am I letting my parents down? Am I letting all of womankind down by resorting to a life that now seems prehistoric? What will my children think of me someday?

I felt snowed-under until I reached a point when I realised that it was MY CHOICE! That is the beauty of the world and the times in which we live. Women now have a choice in how they will live their lives. We can choose to work or we can choose to be home. Yes, some women have no choice but to work in order to provide for their families; just as some women have no choice but to stay at home because they are forced to by their spouses or because they have to look after their children. For those of us who have a choice in the matter, we should be confident in the choice we make. We should live our lives with no regret. We should not judge the next woman for the choices that she has made. As long as we are living according to the laws of Allah as set out in the *Quran* and the *Sunnah* of the *Prophet Muhammad (SAW)* then we have nothing to be ashamed of.

As I write this, it has been three years since I last worked in my profession as a speech therapist. It has also been three years since I began work as a home executive. I now take pride in my home and those that I love by providing a loving environment for them. I have also begun learning more about Islam – an occupation I would never have had time for, had I been caught in the hum drum of work.

I am still me. I am still a powerful, intelligent, intellectual, eloquent, well-educated woman of the 21st century. Domination versus Submission … I have dominated my conflict by submitting to my true calling …

Veils from the past

Anonymous

Apartheid and poverty were the twin challenges facing Fatima, the young Indian widow brought to Cape Town by her now deceased husband. Before he died, he made her promise not to take his children back to India.

But how was she to survive? It was in the nineteen-forties; she was in a strange land, unschooled in English or Afrikaans, with only her domestic skills in making *samoosas* and other knick-knacks to keep her young family alive. True, she still had a roof over her head, left to her by her late husband – with express instructions not to sell it. It took a feisty spirit, entrepreneurial skills, and the overwhelming love of a dedicated mother for her helpless young charges, to see Fatima through those dark days. She taught herself Afrikaans, rented out some of her rooms to tenants, and made *samoosas* which she sold to shops for a living. Kind community members would drop grocery hampers at her door. Ah! Compassion was in good supply in the good old days!

The three surviving children went to a government school and she even managed to send them to a secondary school. However, money was in short supply and two of her sons had to enter the world of work thereafter, while the youngest son furthered his studies. Those were long, hard, gruelling hours for the sons, who were up from six in the morning until eleven at night, battling to make ends meet. They got married, and each son and his young family had to live in a room in the house. Needless to say, the children seldom got a chance to see their fathers.

I am one of the daughters of the eldest surviving son. When our single room could not accommodate the five of us any longer, the family set about looking for a house. A small, affordable house was located in a "coloured" area. We were told not to mention, under any circumstances, the fact that we were Indian and so we moved into our new home, quite unlawfully under the then Group Areas Act. This Act was meant to keep different race groups segregated from each other, and Indians were not allowed to live in a "coloured" area.

So began my life at a "coloured" Calvinistic government school, concealing my Indian identity, falling in with their custom of saying the daily Lord's Prayer, and hymn-singing. It was a Christian-dominated, co-educational culture. My parents could not afford to give us anything else. "Coloured" children would mock us for being *moore*, and I was bullied by them for having straight hair while they had curled hair. It was a nightmare walking home from school with a crowd of children at my heels, ready for a fist-fight. A kindly neighbour took pity on me and informed my mother that children were spoiling for a fight with me. It never occurred to me to complain to my mother about the school problems!

We went to *madressah* after school and read *salaah* since our preteen years – this has been our main anchor in preserving our Islamic identity. Islamic literature was not widely available and the Islamic ethos and culture were not widespread in the sixties and seventies.

I was a shy, introverted girl and took refuge in reading books. Fortunately, a public library was always within walking distance from my home. My love for reading led me to get good grades in secondary school, and I eventually got a scholarship from the then Department of Coloured Affairs to study at university. However, I had to apply for a permit to enter the "white" university in Cape Town, which I managed to get. It was a culture shock of gigantic proportions for me – much worse than school! University seemed to be synonymous with atheism: religion was mocked, ridiculed and belittled. God Himself was derided. The theory of evolution was espoused with great gusto as if it were a fact of life. The life of the Hereafter was "pooh-poohed", and carnal pleasure was the order of the day, with open displays of indecent behaviour and dress-codes.

Depressed and estranged from western culture, I once more hid myself away in my books and, what saved my sanity was, once again, my *salaah* – it anchored me in an otherwise abysmal sea of destruction and depravity from which I could not escape.

My family had absolutely no idea of my traumatic experiences and carried on as normal, completely oblivious to my suffering, loneliness and alienation. There were no other Muslim women in my class and I found myself, once more, a stranger in a foreign culture. However, I managed to pass each year, despite my depressed circumstances, and became a medical professional.

Now I discovered that I had become a hybrid – not fitting in completely with my own culture because of being a professional from a Western university, nor fitting into a Western culture because of my Islam. Once more I felt alone and alienated. Fortunately, my saving grace has been that I am in a profession which helps fellow citizens, so I could relate to all kinds of people in this capacity. By helping others I was, in fact, staying connected to the human race.

But I could not force myself into an arranged marriage, nor could I relate to premarital courting, so I have stayed single and put my trust in my *Creator*, knowing that He who has guided me throughout my life, will also guide my future.

It is my fervent wish that separate educational facilities for girls and boys – right through to university level – be urgently implemented by the Muslim *ummah*, to prevent future generations from becoming alienated from Islam, or from being absorbed into an alien culture. I could not reach my full potential in a co-educational environment, because of my natural shyness. I have had to armour-plate myself psychologically to cope with this Western environment and, as a result, have been forced to distance myself from my natural instincts as a Muslim woman. Islam embraces education – what we need is the correct Islamic environment in which to nurture our youth.

It is now time to test the full strength of South Africa's democracy by realising the full potential of the new twenty-first century generation of youth, both in secular and Islamic studies. In fact, we should not separate the two, because Islam gave rise to the greatest scientists, mathematicians, geographers, astronomers and medical professionals from which the modern world has built its sciences. It is high time that we start the ball rolling again!

Against all odds

Zayboon Motala

Sixty-eight years ago, on the twenty-seventh night of *Ramadaan*, in a small town called Grasmere, fate took a turn. There was joy that lasted only an hour, and then a mother of ten children took her last breath, and was no more. I was my mother's tenth child. I was told that while her janaaza lay in one corner, surrounded by grieving and praying family and friends, I went unnoticed. It was only when I let out a cry that I was nestled against my *Daadi's* bosom, by whom I would be raised. My *Daadi* often said that Allah truly had a hand in my upbringing because as a child I did not suffer with childhood diseases like measles, chicken-pox and mumps. My *Daadi* was a caring and loving granny who instilled beautiful values in me, values for which I am often thankful for. With tear-filled eyes and a deep set sense of longing in my heart, I pray that Allah grant my *Daadi Jannah*, *Aameen*.

I lived together with my *Daadi*, my *Gorabajee*, my *Bibi Fooi* and my cousins Fazila and Rashida in a house on Terrace Road in Fordsburg where the Oriental Plaza now stands. My *Gorabajee* was my guardian and he saw to my basic needs. My *Bibi Fooi*, as my paternal aunt, also played a pivotal role in my upbringing. She would sew the prettiest dresses for me, ideal for a little girl growing up in the 1950's. My *Daadi* believed in doing housework on her own and did not want to keep a helper, so my cousins and I did our share of cleaning every morning before going to school.

My siblings often speak of my mother and tell me what a memorable woman she was. Her second love after her family was the poor African community. She worked tirelessly, and her heart was always with the poorest of the poor. Every winter morning, she would prepare tea and soup for her customers. Aunty Agnes, who visits me from time to time, speaks fondly of my mother and tells me of the love so many had for her. Many of the "white" families shared the same sentiments.

My father, Essop Motala, was a remarkable man. Over weekends, my father would slaughter sheep on his farm, cook big pots of food and people from Evaton, Vereeniging and Johannesburg would come together to eat and socialise. After my mother's death, my father married Amina Moolla and later married his third wife, namely Fatima Motala. May Allah grant them *Jannah Aameen*. I have so many fond memories of my father. I remember how he extended his home by loading bricks in his Fargo and building four rooms and even a Café. We needed a big house, as my father had re-married and we had become a large family – eight sisters and six brothers. I remember how my father took his foot off the accelerator to save petrol and when I am driving, I do the same. Tragedy struck in 1950, when my father lost three sons in a train accident. Allah granted my father patience to be able to bear this great loss.

Eid in Grasmere was special and always buzzing with excitement in my father's big house. My extended family, about two hundred people at times, met to celebrate. Everybody contributed towards the *Eid* lunch. The excitement started days before when the women in the family planned ahead to create delectable dishes. Dressed in their *Eid* best, little ones flaunted the latest fashion trends and compared *mendhi* designs. We would start *Eid* activities after my father and the family men got back from the *kabrastaan*. Although our Grasmere house no longer exists and the elderly have departed from this world, traditional *Eid* gatherings still continue in our family. To this day we look forward to exchanging gifts. I look forward to *Eid-ul-Adha* when sheep arrive a few days earlier and are fed by the young children of the family, up to the day of *Eid* when they are slaughtered. I wait in anticipation to enjoy the fresh sheep liver, that is cooked on *Eid* night for all to enjoy.

From early on, I realised the need to carry on with the *da'wah* work that my mother did, before she passed away. I found my niche in inviting women from other religions to the fold of Islam. In my quest, I successfully managed with the help of Allah, to assist many women and amongst them Gogo Ayesha, a 94 year old woman, to become Muslim. In my interaction with people from other religions, I discovered that I needed to be sincere and honest. The key to bringing people into the fold of Islam is to be a living example in day to day actions.

Besides my involvement in *da'wah* work, I was also involved in the politics of our past, here in South Africa. I was inspired by Aunty

(Dr) Zainab Asvat, a freedom fighter and activist. Many years ago, on the 9th of August 1956, now recognised as "National Women's Day", I, dressed in white, was amongst the twenty thousand women who staged a march on the Union Buildings in Pretoria to protest against the proposed amendments to the Urban Areas Act (commonly known as the pass laws) of 1950. We all sang a protest song together that was composed in honour of the occasion: *Wathint'Abafazi Wathint'imbokodo*! The police chased us … dogs got at my lovely white dress … and my eyes swelled with tears. The day was eventful and up to today I still feel proud that I was part of this historical event. I sang, chanted, marched and ran all in the name of freedom. It all came to an end when evening fell, but that day remains in my mind and in the minds and hearts of others, when we re-live memories of our march to freedom every year on the 9th August.

Another early recollection is that of a political meeting which took place on the Red Square, which was opposite our home. Red Square was our haven where we as children played marbles, five stones and all sorts of other games. We looked forward to that time of year, when the "white man" brought his merry-go-round to the Square. It was a treat for us and yet a dark parody. For all the political meetings that took place on the Red Square, the police came out in full force. On one particular day, some several activists sought refuge in our home, while others scaled walls, running for their dear lives into people's yards and homes. Not long thereafter, there was a loud banging on our front door. My *Daadi*, in her broken Afrikaans, looked through the window and enquired, "*Ja, wat jy soek?*" The policeman cheekily asked, "*Waar is die mense?*" My *Daadi* called me to her side and answered, "*Ek en die kind is mense.*" This went on until the policeman got fed-up and moved on to the next house. That evening, a number of activists were picked up and taken to John Vorster Square. Being young and vulnerable, my heart would pound whenever I heard the thumping of a policeman's boots.

I smile when I remember how for the first time in South African history, the possibility of a Black African President was more than just a dream. People from all walks of life were scared, but the negative became a positive for many. In 1990, Nelson Mandela was released from the shackles into freedom. I had accompanied my friend Ayesha

Khota and her family to the Jabulani Theatre in Soweto. As there were no TV screens, we listened to the Master of Ceremonies doing a count down from ten to the moment when "*Madiba*" stepped out of Pollsmoor prison. The atmosphere was magical – crowds cheered, sang and cried. It was deafening, and it seemed as though the ground was vibrating. For me in my heart, as a nation, we had finally taken the long walk to freedom.

In the September of 1969, I embarked on the great pilgrimage of *Hajj* with my father. We went for four and a half months and only returned home in mid February of the year 1970. We spent the first few weeks in Medina, the final resting place of our beloved Prophet Muhammad (*SAW*). It is a city of peace and tranquility. We were fortunate to do many tours and were shown the ground where Bibi Fatima's (*RA*) house stood and the spot where Prophet Muhammad's (*SAW*) camel stopped. I also managed to eat a date from the tree that Prophet Muhammad (*SAW*) had planted. In those days well-wishers from home would always ask *Haajis* to bring *Khaakhi shifa. Khaakhi shifa* was a hillock then but today it's a hollow ground over which a bridge has been constructed. *Makkah* the city of Prophet Muhammad's (*SAW*) birth still retains a very close place in my heart and is filled with memories that are engraved there forever. Seeing the *Kaaba* for the first time was an emotional experience which I am sure many can relate to. I was given the opportunity of taking a few stitches on the cover of the *Holy Kaaba* for the coming year. During that trip we women used to pray our *salaah* on pebbles on the mataaf area. From the haram overlooking the Kaaba was *Hazrat* Bilaal's *masjid.* Many of the historical sites have been broken, only to be replaced by modern high rise buildings.

I cannot thank the Almighty enough for having invited me to His house in those years to make maximum benefit of my *Hajj* trip. Almost every *tahajjud* we would go down to the *well of Zam Zam* and the guard would draw the water up from the well. After having our fill we would leave the well site drenched and thereafter my father would give the gate keeper something in his hand as a token of appreciation.

It was truly amazing to watch millions of people praying at the same time and following the same rituals together, for the pleasure of Allah. During *Hajj* there was no differentiation between rich or poor, fair or dark skinned; everybody was equal in their journey and reason for being there. In *Hajj* I found a great sense of spirituality. I felt the presence of my Allah in my prayer. Today, I am thankful that I fulfilled my obligation to Allah, by performing my first *Hajj* when I could walk and climb easily.

After the passing of my *Daadi*, in 1976, I resigned from the school where I taught and visited my maternal grandmother in Barbados. My *Nanima* got married in 1915 and moved to Barbados where she lived until she passed away. During the apartheid era it was difficult to obtain a visa but the Ambassador of Barbados in London was a family friend and therefore made it easier for me to obtain entry into the country. My first meeting with my *Nanima* was one of immense happiness. My *Nanima*, who was 94 years old at the time, came to the airport to meet me. On our way to my aunt's home my *Nanima* kept touching me. For both of us it was a dream come true. She repeatedly said, "Is this my Rookeya's baby child?" I was her only grandchild from my ten siblings that my *Nanima* got to meet. My *Nanima* would take me for a walk around and proudly say in her *Bajan* accent, "Meet my daughter's daughter from Africa." I spent five long months with my *Nanima*, my aunt, my uncle and their lovely family in Barbados. Only when I was told my visa could no longer be extended did I leave with a heavy heart and the next day in Venezuela I came down with fever. Six years later, my grandmother departed from this world, leaving sweet, dear memories.

I attended primary school in Fietas and madressa at Newtown *madressah*. After completing high school, I went to college to study teaching. In those days, nursing and teaching were the only two careers opened to Indians. I began teaching at the Ferreira's Town School in 1964, and thereafter taught at Lenasia High and Park Primary. In 1976, when the Soweto Riots broke out, I was in Barbados, in the West Indies. It was then that my family encouraged me to get a teaching post in either Canada or Brazil. I chose to teach in Brazil and was there for six months when on one fateful evening, I met with a car accident which left me physically disabled. The accident opened up a new dimension in my life and allowed me to view my contemporaries in a different light. Before the accident, I failed to take notice of the needs of physically challenged people. I initially felt terribly guilty, but as time passed, I blanked these thoughts out of my mind, always thanking Allah for all the blessings I enjoyed, as there were those who were far worse off than what I was. For eleven long years, I could not walk and for the nine months that a cast was wrapped around my body, my sister-in-law Fatima and my sister Sabera bathed me and assisted me in every way possible. My friends and family were very supportive during that trying time in my life and I am always thankful for them. My brother Basheer, my sister-in-law Fatima, and my sister Sabera played pivotal roles in my life in those years. They were indeed my pillars of strength.

I consider every setback a challenge. My courage and strength came from my firm belief in my Allah as my guide and protector. I believe the path of life is hard and nobody is immune to difficulties. Life is a test from Allah and my sincere supplication to Allah was my only solace. I found peace in recitation of the *Quran,* fasting and salaah. My journey during those eleven years, allowed me to discover the power of *duah* – the key to changing our lives. For me there was light at the end of the tunnel, I just needed to be very patient and have total faith in my *Creator.*

During the 11 years of disability, I underwent 18 operations but as a physically challenged person, I achieved a lot more than I did before the accident. I got my firearm and driving licenses. I served on a number of committees, took up cake decorating, flower arranging and fabric painting as well as studied a number of courses including early childhood development. I always kept myself busy. I spent two years in a hospital bed and during that time my *da'wah* work continued. I spoke to the nurses and other hospital staff about our beautiful religion. I was often wheeled to the children's ward where I entertained the patients with stories. In the Occupational Therapy room, I carried out craft workshops with the patients, and during the festive season, I made flower arrangements to decorate the wards at Coronation Hospital.

In May of 1987, *Alhamdullilah*, I started walking again, and another chapter of my life opened. I walked with a severe limp, but that did not deter me from carrying on. As an educator, I realised that some schools were not well managed. There were many de-motivated and unqualified teachers in schools. In my own small way I set the ball rolling. Just beyond Roshnee is Damfontein, a farming area with a humble settlement owned by Mrs Brown. I spoke to her, and there I started a pre-school under a tree. I taught there for 18 months. One day, my car with all my educational material, got stolen. I was not deterred, I persevered and soon after, we began receiving many donations which gave us the incentive to carry on. An electric company situated in Meyerton donated a zozo. Later on, Mr Saloojee built a classroom, and things became better. Johannesburg City Council donated a double-decker bus. For years I personally undertook the effort of cooking a rice dish, twice a week, for the learners and their families. I felt inner peace and gratification at the end of each day.

Our noble Prophet Muhammad (*SAW*) said, "Closest to the Almighty are those who are most useful to his dependants." My calling was to help others; so, soon after I started working, I started the Tomahole, Tsuneng Centre for the Physically Challenged in Parys. We started off with just one physically challenged person in one room and only many years later we moved to a municipal building. Today, Tsuneng Centre for the Physically Challenged boasts its own place. Through monies donated by companies, we managed to purchase the site and building which is used today. Themba, the chairman, has done a phenomenal job. Themba is wheelchair-bound, but he is the master-mind behind the success of the centre. He also spearheads obtaining hundreds of low-cost housing units. Mr Saloojee also, over the years, donated refrigerators, sewing machines and specially designed cots for patients who had cerebral palsy. In 2008, I was invited to a ribbon cutting ceremony in Parys where a school was named after me, namely "The Zayboon Motala School for the Physically Challenged". Later in subsequent years, Nelson Mandela, the president of South Africa at the time, visited me at the Roshnee Nursery Pre-School. I felt honoured and grateful to my Allah for granting me the ability to help others.

Subsequently, I also opened the Al Huda Pre-School in Ironsyde, as well as two schools in Malawi where I conduct classes to empower women. Together with Hawa Dhorat we often go to Malawi to distribute Ramadan hampers to the poor Muslims there. Sister Hawa has also set up agricultural farms there, and in this way, we empower people to become self-sufficient, and as the Chinese proverb goes, "Give a man a fish and you feed him for a day. Teach a man to fish and you feed him for a lifetime." Having been a member of Toastmasters International, and giving coaching in Speech and Craft courses, a friend encouraged me to start the Al-Huda Magazine. It was not long thereafter that I joined as a presenter on Radio Islam, a part-time activity which I enjoyed tremendously.

It was in my fifth year as presenter on Radio Islam, that I adopted Julia Nomsa Sihlongonyane (Zuleikha). I resigned at the radio station because I needed to be home to welcome my daughter when she came home from school. Zuleikha's mother Emily, worked for my late sister Zuleikha Motala Sayanvala. Two days before her death, she left her three children in my sister's care, and asked her to bring them into the fold of Islam. My sister, being the philanthropist she was, gladly took these children under her wing. My daughter, Julie, as I fondly call her, also lost her father when she was six years old. When I met my dear Julie for the first time, I could see the sadness in her eyes and I made *duah* to Allah to help me remove her pain. Zuleikha had to change from a rural lifestyle to an urban lifestyle with Indians. *Alhamdulillah*, today she is a confident young *Aalima* who is conversant in both Urdu and Arabic while I myself am still struggling to understand the Arabic tongue.

I married late in life. I lived an independent life until Mohamed Areington came into it. I married at the age of sixty, fulfilling a *sunnah* of our dear Prophet Muhammad (*SAW*). I found a ready-made family of two wonderful daughters, two sisters-in-law, eight sons, eight daughters-in-law, twenty-nine grandchildren and two great-grandchildren. But fate once again took a roundabout turn when my dear husband passed, leaving me with only memories of a beautiful but short-lived marriage. I realised that the bond of marriage is very different to every other, as whether one is married for a month, a year or fifty years, losing a partner is one of the hardest experiences to accept. I learned a lot from my husband, especially when it came to

Islamic knowledge. I thank the Almighty for blessing me with a man of my husband's calibre. I know he is smiling down on me as I write my thoughts of him. May Mohamed, all my dear and near ones, and everyone else be rewarded with high places in *Jannah, Aameen.*

After forty-six years in education, I now spend my retirement reading, assisting the Vaal Muslim Women's Forum and helping on the Tomahole and Malawi projects. I am also involved in a beginners' craft book for younger learners. I need to carry on and I thank Allah for giving me the strength and ability to do so. I've realised through my life's journey that my true purpose in living is to help others and that for me is my quest – to find those in need.

“Not a suitable career for a young Muslim girl”

Jasmine Khan

“Not a suitable career for a young Muslim girl.” This was the second time these words were uttered by my father, this time because an aptitude test recommended journalism as a career for me. Strangely the second pronouncement did not upset me as much as the first one had. Even though I had indulged in scribbling up to that point in my life, journalism was a foreign concept that had not even entered my mind. At the age of nineteen, I was still focused on becoming a nurse. Looking back now, I cannot imagine why: I still freeze at the sight of blood.

Against all logic, from the time I first became interested in deciding what I wanted in life, my dream was to become a nurse. Maybe it had to do with the stories of Florence Nightingale that I read as a child. Whatever it was, I held firm to my dream and ambition. Sadly, it was not to be. When I finished Standard Six and told my parents I wanted to be a nurse, my father first used the phrase, “Not a suitable career for a young Muslim girl.” This was during the 1950s, and opportunities for non-whites to pursue a further education were limited. Besides, the only two professions open to me were teaching and nursing. Often I think that I chose nursing simply because teaching did not appeal to me. I had to choose one of the two because my passion was learning, I wanted to study further, and ending my school career at age thirteen was not an option.

When I was thirteen, children were still children, and parents held absolute sway over their children. In addition to this, my father was a dyed-in-the-wool Indian, and the idea of girls studying further was not to be considered. I was told that I should become a dressmaker, another “suitable” profession for a girl. This was laughable since I hated a needle and thread, and, even today, can hardly sew on a button. My idea of shortening a garment is to just double the existing hem and use stitches that look like a spider gone mad.

So there I was, confined to the house with nothing to do. Once my chores were completed I would lock myself in my bedroom and read. I was a voracious reader, reading everything from comic books, weekly magazines to books which I am sure my mother would have not considered suitable. I remember coming across a sealed carton in our storeroom. Upon opening it I found it filled with magazines belonging to my grandmother. They were British magazines and I pounced upon them like an addict. Six months passed like this, me locked in my room and reading, and my mother getting more and more impatient with me.

Finally, she did something totally out of character, and for which I am eternally grateful. I pray that Allah grants her the highest stage in *Jannah, Insha'Allah*. She asked her brother's wife to take me to the nearest high school for enrolment. Alas, the Principal refused to take me, pointing out that it was the end of the second term, and the year was half gone. Another disappointment! That night my dear mother did something else which was totally out of character. She had gone against my father's wishes to send me to the school, and I fully expected that she would keep quiet about it. No, she very bravely told my father. This is where I got another shock. Instead of getting angry at my mother; my father adopted the attitude of "how dare this Principal refuse to take my daughter as is". The next morning he went off to the school and two hours later he and Mr Braam were firm friends, and I was to be allowed to start school the next term.

However, there was a condition attached. I was not allowed to write the end of year exam, and would remain in standard seven the following year. This did not bother me; I was in seventh heaven. It is not in my nature to coast along comfortably, besides I was far too excited to be back at school. I applied myself to the school work and at the end of the year all my teachers petitioned the Principal. They felt that I deserved to be given a chance since I had worked so diligently. He agreed, once again with a proviso, that I would not go to standard eighr the following year, I would have to repeat the year. This was because in those days standard's seven and eight formed what was known as Junior Certificate, and most of the syllabus was covered in the first year, the second half of the second year being taken up with revision of the previous year's work. Thus the principal's decision was to protect me, and not out of malice. To cut a long story short, I wrote the examination and in spite of high marks in all other subjects,

I failed needlework. I obtained practically 100% in the theory of the paper, but, no surprise, failed the practical. I also failed mathematics, another subject I was never good at. Once again the teachers petitioned the principal to promote me to standard eight, and once again he relented.

I found myself at the age of fifteen the proud possessor of a Junior Certificate, and really believed that I could now proceed to Conradie Hospital as nurse's aide until I reached the age of eighteen. This was the minimum age to enter the training programme for nurses. My father, in cahoots with Mr Braam, had other ideas. My achievement of completing a two year course in eighteen months showed that my future lay in academia, and it would be wasted on emptying bedpans. So off I went for another two years to obtain my Senior Certificate. Fortunately, both mathematics and needlework left my life. Although I loved school, and the learning process, I still dreamt of being a nurse, but I had to wait for this dream, or should I say, nightmare, to become a reality.

After finishing high school at seventeen, the powers that be, in this case my father and another school principal, decided that I must go to university. I have to say that in spite of being pushed along the path of higher education, I was not unhappy. I loved my year and a bit at the University of Cape Town, studying history and English, but something was still driving me towards nursing. I do believe my father eventually gave in out of sheer desperation, so in 1960 I entered Somerset Hospital as a trainee nurse. I am not going to dwell too much on that period, except to say that as happy as I was at the hospital, I was desperately unhappy at home. There were circumstances at home that year which caused great confusion. When I was at the hospital I longed to be home, and when I was at home I could not take what was happening and I would long to be back at the hospital. The strain finally took its toll and one morning I found myself sitting on my bed at home, clutching a purse in one hand and a handkerchief in the other. Sitting opposite me was my brother, with tears in his eyes. Apparently, I had disappeared from my room at the hospital; the last person to see me was my roommate when she left for breakfast at 06.00. The matron called my father and he reported me missing to the police. I was totally unaware of all this, and until today I do not know where I was for those hours. I was sent to a psychologist and she did an aptitude test. This is where the result came that the profession I was best suited to was journalism and that's when my father made his second pronouncement that it was not a suitable profession for a Muslim girl.

After my breakdown I put all thoughts of nursing out of my mind. This is the period when I turned to putting my thoughts to paper. Still not with any idea of becoming a writer, I just found it cathartic to express my feelings on paper. Even today, when someone comes to me for help, I recommend writing down what you feel, because by doing so your pain and trauma becomes once-removed. I cannot honestly say that what the psychologist said influenced me; the thought of becoming a journalist did not even register on my radar. It was too far-fetched a concept. What did happen is that I turned more and more to writing, mostly about what was happening to me. I also had a very vivid imagination, and I would spend hours constructing a scenario in minute detail, even to the exact placing of furniture. Strangely enough I never considered fiction. I found it easier to look at a situation and comment on it.

Years passed. I did not go back to nursing, or to university. After a course in hairdressing I worked in my own salon for several years. After that I entered the secretarial world armed with a course in shorthand and typing. After I got married I continued with office work, until I became interested in librarianship. While living in Kimberley I still continued my reading and used to watch the staff when I visited the public library. One day I asked the person in charge what qualification is need to work in the library, and she said "a matric certificate". I started my career as a librarian in Kimberley, and on my return to Cape Town I applied successfully for a post with city libraries. It was while talking to the head of the library where I worked, that my life took another turn. He was telling me one day that in his opinion I should take up my interrupted studies. When I told him that I could not afford to do so, he explained the concept of long-distance studying through Unisa, where you can study one course per year. When I heard that the requirement for a degree was ten courses, I exclaimed, "Heavens, it will take me ten years." His reply will always be etched in my memory, "Yes my dear, but if you do not do it, the ten years will pass anyway, and you will have nothing to show for it." At this point my marriage was going steadily downhill, and I felt that studying would help me. Accordingly I registered for a B.A. at Unisa at age fourty-four. It took me nine years, but only seven of studying, to complete my degree. This was during the height of the 80's unrest. I travelled to work in buses without windows which had to traverse roads where tires were burning. In addition I was worried about my children's safety because of the unrest in the schools.

It was during this traumatic period that I began writing seriously, and trying to get my work published. I wrote a novel about the unrest, but it was rejected by a publisher. I also started writing articles, two of which were accepted for publication by mainstream magazines. In 1990 I won a national short story competition run by the African Writers Association. A year later my marriage finally broke down completely, and my sons and I moved. Although I wanted to write and be published, I felt that neither I, nor my writing, was good enough. Even with the success during 1990, I lacked the confidence to pursue my writing further. To a certain extent it was rekindled in 1996 when I worked for the Boorhaanol Islam Movement. They published a magazine, and it was my task to get the articles in on time. I even wrote a few articles for the magazine. However, it was to be another nine years before the words of the psychologist would resound with me again.

I retired in 2002, and in 2004 I experienced a journey of self-discovery, both literal and figurative. During 2005 I wrote a Personal Growth Programme titled "Positive Energy Guide to Perfect Emotional Grace", PEG for short. I partnered up with a parenting expert the following year, and for four years we did Islamic parenting and self-awareness workshops in the community. I then became aware of the trauma and unhappiness amongst our women. An article on the abuse of a woman in Gauteng prompted me to send a letter to the editor of *Muslim Views*. This resulted in my writing the column "stop the cycle", commenting on what is happening in the community, and giving guidelines according to the *Quran* and *sunnah*. The column ran for three years, and I now write under another title *From Consciousness to Contentment.*

Five years after writing the original manuscript I decided to have a look at it. This was prompted by the amazing feedback I got to the "stop the cycle" articles, from as far afield as Norway, Lebanon and New Zealand. I figured that the gestation period was long enough, time to call in the midwife. Five years had passed and I had grown and developed, so the manuscript had to be redone. I was by now very determined that this book would be published. It chronicles my journey, and I had this absolute conviction that it must be available in order to help others. I decided to self-publish but had no money. All my attempts at getting help were fruitless, but I knew that Allah would open the way. Finally, the manuscript was done, edited by two separate persons, and painstakingly proofread by my son and myself. Still without a cent, the book was published and launched on 10th Muharram (16th December) 2010. Exactly fifty years after the result of an aptitude test I had taken at the age of nineteen.

At the end of six weeks the book had sold enough copies to pay for the design and layout and a month later the printing costs were covered. Thus far the book has sold 1400 copies. My second book, *Behind Closed Doors* was released after. The book is a compilation of the "stop the cycle" articles. It is not just a collection of the articles. They have been arranged to flow into a narrative, which asks the question, "How are we living in the light of the *Quran* and *Sunnah*?"

I am truly grateful to my *Creator*, Allah, that I was able to publish my first book at the age of sixty-nine, with wisdom. I end my life story with a message to all my sisters out there, "Never despair of the mercy of Allah, and what Allah has decreed for you, will come to you." Thus far I am grateful to Allah that my books have helped so many people out there.

My journey into spiritual awakening

Tazmin Mahomed

I was forty years of age when my eyes opened to the reality of the purpose of my existence. Up to that point in my life, I had nurtured relationships with my family, friends and acquaintances, but my relationship with my *Creator* had fallen short. I sensed a huge void in my soul and this void was created solely because I had not brought *Him* into my life. I regarded myself as a practicing Muslim – I prayed, fasted, went for *Hajj* and *Umrah,* but I had never gone that extra mile. I viewed myself as a philosophical person purely because I loved reading books by Deepak Chopra, Wayne Dyer, Paolo Coelho, Rumi, Kahlil Gibran and many other such authors, convinced that I was on the path to filling the void. As the restlessness within my soul continued to escalate, I understood that I had been duping only myself and that I was nowhere near to finding the truth.

I took a small initial step, by trying to attend more Islamic talks and by taking a course in *tajweed*, to improve my recitation of the *Quran*. I wanted to change but was too afraid, fearing that I would not like a "holy" me. Despite this fear, my soul was thirsty and I tried to quench this thirst with whatever Islamic knowledge I could get my hands on. The change at this point was purely internal: my thoughts were changing but my actions remained the same. Externally I appeared the same – I rarely covered my hair in public aside from occasions that deemed it necessary to do so, such as funerals and religious gatherings. Designer clothes, heels, suits and highlighted hair were the order of the day. Despite this, I felt stuck in a rut, doing mundane things, day in and day out, getting nowhere. Deep down, I knew that there was something missing from my life. There was nothing materially lacking in my world but I felt hugely unfulfilled and incomplete. As the void in my soul got deeper, the thirst within me grew more intense.

As a Muslim woman living in a "western" society, I found it much harder to cover up and assume my Islamic identity. For those women living in an Islamic country, covering up is a much less daunting task as it is a social obligation for them. In our country, *hijab* is a personal choice and Muslim women are free to decide whether to cover or not to cover their hair. This freedom, ironically, posed a severe restriction for me. I chose to fit into the mainstream mould. I did this purely because my faith was not strong enough and because of a deep-rooted insecurity and fear. I needed to wear the mask of vanity. Holding on to this mask gave me a sense of "security". I chose to follow rather than to lead and internalised society's lie, which tells us that "the younger you look, the happier you will be and the more socially accepted you will feel". I strove relentlessly to perfect my outer shell, sadly, at the expense of my soul. This relentless chasing would only lead to me to a dead-end as I clearly understood that, as hard as I tried, I would never be "thin enough, young enough or fashionable enough". I could feel myself getting caught in a macabre material chase, which was getting me nowhere and was giving me no self-fulfillment. I knew that I needed to steer my life in a different direction!

A few weeks short of my forty-third birthday, I reached a turning point when attending a ladies-only spiritual retreat weekend, the theme of which was purification of the heart – *Tazkiya*. The retreat teacher spoke directly to my heart. As she spoke, I went numb; I went into shock because I acknowledged that I had been spiritually sleeping and that it was my *Creator* who was missing from my life. This thought sent shivers down my spine. I began to question my actions. What type of Muslim is too afraid to look like one in public? Can a true believer disobey so blatantly? My *Creator* had ordained me to cover my hair and I had consciously disobeyed. I felt so ashamed of myself. I viewed myself as an insincere believer, a hypocrite. As I reflected I wrote these words … "This heart is numb, this heart is hard, this heart is smeared, this heart is black". As the teacher spoke about the diseases of the heart, I came to the grim realisation that mine was indeed diseased and not clean, as I had previously assumed it to be. I had previously justified not covering my hair by saying that my heart is clean, so it did not matter whether or not I covered my hair in public.

I understood that I needed to change. "Now or Never," I wrote! If I could not change after hearing the blatant truth then I would never change! I knew that I had to awaken myself from my spiritual slumber and acknowledge that I was in dire need of what my teacher referred to as a "spiritual shower". I began to question my love for my *Creator*, to question where *He* stood in my life and what priority did I give *Him*? If I truly loved *Him*, would I have not obeyed *Him*? How could I have been so proud and arrogant? Thoughts raced through my mind, the more I thought, the more ashamed I became and I felt an urgent desire to remain covered up. It was as if I had been caught out. I knew that I had to stop playing games with my *Creator*. I acknowledged that I had succumbed to the fool's paradise and had been denying myself the opportunity of gaining true paradise, by obeying my Lord. My teacher never mentioned the word "scarf" or "*hijab*", she spoke about Allah's Mercy and His Greatness. She said, "Do not fear Allah but be overwhelmed by Him, be in awe of Him." I soon realised that I am nothing and that Allah is everything. I slowly reached the point of surrender and made a sincere prayer asking my Lord to give me the strength to cover my hair and to change my life and my focus. I used to think that it was "just a headscarf"; I now understood that it is more than that. It is a symbol of my love for Allah, a symbol of submission and surrender … no more pride … no more excuses … no more holding back.

We learn from an early age that Allah is omnipresent, omnipotent and omniscient. I had only just begun to understand these concepts. I had never truly acknowledged that my *Creator* is everywhere, and that is why I had found it so easy to disobey such an important command. In taking the step of covering my hair, I knew that I had crossed a major threshold and at the same time, I experienced a huge sense of relief. I had freed myself from the guilt of disobedience and had simultaneously submitted myself to my *Creator* as I had consciously decided to put *Him* before fashion and vanity. Pleasing *Him* has become my sole purpose. My headscarf is now glued to my head. It is an external symbol of the internal change that occurred within my heart. It is a constant reminder that my *Creator* is closer to me than my jugular vein. It serves as a protective shield and encourages me to be humble. Most importantly, it has given me a newfound self-confidence and sense of security. Every time I wear the headscarf, I experience what I call, "Scarf Magic". I feel transformed the moment I drape this piece of cloth around my head. This same piece of cloth that has become a symbol of hate, disdain and oppression around the globe, to me represents a symbol of freedom – freedom from the shackles of fashion, vanity, arrogance and pride. Instead of oppressing me, it liberates me, instead of making me look like a "granny." it makes me feel like a true beauty queen.

When I went home after the retreat, I continued to reflect and as I did so, words just poured out of me. It felt as if the floodgates of understanding had opened up and I could not stop myself from composing poems and writing reflections. I retreated into a corner of my room and poured my heart out. I had to release all the darkness within my heart in order to see the light, to feel the light and to let this light shine within me. I acted as one who has just fallen in love and my days were spent walking around in a daze, almost like in a drunken stupor. I had lost interest in all material things around me and found solace only in my prayer and my poetry. I reconnected with the poet within me, the poet that I had left behind in my school classroom many years ago. I retreated into myself but I discovered an ocean of hidden gems and treasures. I felt hugely self-satisfied and secure, experiencing a sense of belonging, knowing that I had arrived at the place where I had been created to be.

This deep sense of inner peace and serenity was perceived only because I had invited my *Creator* into my heart. I experienced a physical change within my heart and within my entire being. The heart that I went into the retreat with was hard and numb, this one was, soft and porous, and it felt humbled and ashamed … completely different and brand new. This heart had been infused with a special light of understanding and as a result, I felt like one who had gone for *Hajj* or *Umrah*. I experienced the feeling of *Arafat* yet I had not traveled far, only a few miles north of my home. The experience was exhilarating as it was one that I had been yearning for throughout my adult life.

Within a month of the retreat I had compiled an entire collection of poems and essays describing my journey and reflecting my feelings. I wrote these words purely for the sake of my own catharsis. They were my written contract with my *Creator*; once they were down on paper, they were evidence that this change was genuine. There was no going back now! I wrote to convince myself that my transformation was honest and sincere. I hoped that if ever I turned my back on this journey, then these words would be my saviour. I wrote these words purely for my own private self, never imagining that they would soon be shared!

I mentioned my writing to Elle, a school friend of mine who was a writer by profession. She was keen on reading my work and hearing more about my journey. I needed to share these words and knew that she would understand, as she has known me since the tender age of eleven. She knew the person that I was before marriage and kids. She knew the ambitious me, the free-spirited me and most importantly, she knew the poet me. Occasionally, she would dare to ask me if I was truly happy in my role as mother, housewife, cook and taxi driver. I invariably assured her that I was indeed happy, but deep down I knew that I was disappointed as I had had greater ambitions for myself.

Although I have an Honour's degree in Psychology, I never practiced my profession as I did not get to the stage of Masters. I did however do some volunteer counseling to keep in touch with my studies and on occasion I helped my husband out in his business. But essentially, I remained a stay-at-home mum at the beck and call of my family. As the years went by, I started to believe that I had let down that high achiever within me from high school days. I dreamt of becoming a doctor and of doing big things with my life but had settled very comfortably into my role as wife and mother. On the surface I never had any huge regrets as I had been blessed with a wonderful husband and four precious kids but, every so often, I would get the feeling that I could have done much more with my life. I knew that I needed to be more than just "a wife and a mum".

I had lost complete touch with the person I once was. My only link to that self was Elle, who convinced me to publish the words that I had written. I remember telling her that I knew that many women sitting on the same threshold would relate to the words that I had written. I told her that if I could inspire only one woman then I would have felt as if the effort in publishing would have been worthwhile. My friend owned her own publishing company, which I only discovered on the morning that I visited her and shared my file of poems with her. I told her that Allah had kept her in my life for this reason only … so that one day she would become my publisher!

Many authors take years to publish. "It is not as easy as it seems," authors always tell you. I am truly grateful that Allah made it so easy for me. My husband was willing to pay for the publishing despite business constraints. Elle took the file away from me about six weeks after the retreat and within two months the book was launched at the Cape Town Book Fair. The entire experience was so overwhelming that at times, it felt almost surreal. For the first time in a very long time, I experienced the liberating feeling of doing something entirely by myself and for me but knowing full well that none of this would have happened had I not turned to my *Creator*. Throughout this journey He has been both my muse and my guide. I was truly grateful to Him and only Him, as He had given me so much more than I had bargained for. I had leaped from the domain of housewife to the domain of author within a few months, traveling around the country doing book launches and giving speeches. I finally felt that I was doing something more with my life and serving a higher purpose, knowing full well that this was happening only because of Allah. I could truly relate to the wisdom behind the *Hadith* related by Bukhari, a Muslim, that states, "If my servant draws near to Me at a hand's span, I draw near to him at an arm's length, If he draws near to Me at an arm's length, I draw near to him at a fathom's length and if he comes to Me walking, I go to him running."

I truly felt as if my *Creator* had come running in my direction despite me having taken only a small step towards Him. He is indeed the most merciful and the most generous. I needed to realise that the headscarf is not just an option, but an obligation. It is a passport to liberation, to safety, to modesty, to piety and to protection. Somebody once asked me regarding the headscarf, "Does a piece of cloth have the power to transform?" I truly believe that not only does it have the power to transform but also the power to perform miracles. When hearts transform then miracles happen. The book that Allah made me so easily write and publish is one such miracle. It was written purely from the heart and it is meant to speak to hearts. I am grateful to my *Creator* for opening up my heart, for speaking to it and for allowing me to be infused with words and thoughts and thus enabling me to reconnect with the writer within me.

The entire experience has been both life-changing and liberating. Previously, my identity had always been shaped by other people. I was someone's mother, wife, daughter, sister, daughter-in-law or sister-in-law. After having launched my book, however, I was able to firmly assert my own identity. For the first time since school days I stood on my own and was recognised for my own talent. I finally experienced the feeling of being worth something more. I still fitted into all my previous roles but I now had the added title of "author" and "poet" and had acquired a new soul mate in my *Creator*. This milestone is one that has infused me with a newfound zest for life and living. I am grateful that I was able to experience this transformation.

As overwhelming as the entire experience of launching a book was for me, so was it for my family members. It took them a while to adjust to my new identity. They supported me if what I did, did not impinge on my duty towards them. To them I will always be mum and wife. Most of the time during my busy period of traveling around the country, they saw my leap into the author's domain as just another hobby that I had embarked upon, without allowing themselves to get carried away. This was a blessing in disguise as it helped to keep my ego at bay by forcing me to remain humble and down-to-earth. I never wanted my family to feel that they now took second place in my life. As much as I enjoyed the experience, I always understood that my duty of being a mother would always take precedence over any other role.

For a few months after the launch, wherever I went I was identified as "the woman who wrote that book". This usually made me feel slightly uncomfortable but at the same time it gave me a sense of accomplishment and purpose. Many women wrote to me or messaged me saying that they had been inspired and had started wearing the headscarf after reading the book. Once again I could thank only the Almighty. I truly believed that I had only been used to get those words out there. Throughout the journey, I did not claim a sense of ownership to the book as I had convinced myself that it came through me but not from me.

People forget and life goes on. As the saying goes "yesterday's newspaper headline is today's fish and chips wrapper". I have settled comfortably into this "new" identity, getting used to being called *appa* or *Khala* by car-guards and cashiers. At times I am treated with more respect and at other times with suspicion and contempt. In society at large, some see me as a brainless and oppressed woman while others revere me in the same manner as they would a nun. I personally have reached a point in my life wherein I really do not care what others think of me. As long as my *Creator* is pleased with me then I will be truly happy.

After my book launch, I believed that I had come full circle. I now understand that the circle is never complete as it continues to spiral upwards. There is so much knowledge to acquire, and there are so many books to read, words to write, supplications to learn, talks to attend, people to meet, friends to make and miles to travel.

The more I know, the more I realise how much I do not know, and the more I realise what an insignificant speck my existence is compared to the vastness of the universe.

This journey has now only begun …

From the depths of my soul

Saffiya Ismail

Searching for Answers

As the Sufis say,
"The more you look for Almighty, the more you find yourself."

YES! I was born Muslim!

Being Muslim meant I had to practice and behave in a certain manner. I knew I was different to other girls my age. In school I interacted with mostly Muslim girls, to save myself from answering questions to which I didn't know the answers myself. I went to an all-girls' School, and I knew the hymns from "The Lord is my Shepherd" to "*hava nagila*". We were educated mostly by white, Christian ladies. We had to conform to wearing knee-length dresses, with knee-high socks. In high school, the parents fought for Muslim girls to be allowed to wear pants with their dresses. It was a major event, considering we were schooled in the Apartheid era, and in a non-Islamic environment. At that time, there were no Muslim based schools.

In the afternoons, after school; I went to *madressah*, but everything we read or recited was in Arabic, so I couldn't understand what I was learning. I just blindly parroted verses and memorised prayers, which were meaningless to me. You could have taught me this in French or Spanish and it wouldn't have made a difference. If you didn't learn your prescribed work, you were given corporal punishment. I have the scars to show for it. I actually hated going sometimes. It was rigid and unforgiving. The males were staunch, you could not ask questions and you had to simply follow.

After much persuasion and with the help of my brothers, my mother decided that I attend private Islamic classes with a female teacher. I must confess that this was so different from the rigidity of the *moulanas* at my previous *madressah*. Thankfully this was more interactive and less embarrassing for us as young girls; we didn't get "a slap" in front of boys. Make no mistake, she was also very disciplined and strict about learning, but she was amazing. We would have discussions about "girl stuff", especially as we developed into young ladies, and here she helped us with the questions we were afraid to ask our mothers and aunts.

My mother was so steadfast, something I am sure my grandparents had instilled in her. She made sure she wore a headscarf when she left the home, she fasted as instructed, and she would complete one chapter of the *Quran* every morning at *Fajr* prayer time. She did this every day for as long as I can remember until her last six weeks in hospital. I think my mother probably lost count of how many times she completed reciting the *Quran* in its entirety in her lifetime. I recall my mother and aunts reciting the *Quran* with such sweetness. They were so disciplined.

In my early years I merely acted out what I was expected to do. I had to follow the norm. I had no real connection, so I merely mimicked all that had been taught and displayed to me by family, elders and religious teachers.

Despite all of these sterling examples of faith, I still did not feel that which I yearned to feel. I felt ashamed and guilty for harbouring such thoughts and feelings. I couldn't dare share what I was feeling or thinking, for fear of what my family or those close to me would think. Would they see me as someone who wanted to leave my faith, or would they see me as a rebellious young woman? There were times I felt that I was heading to hell on a first-class ticket.

In my late teens I attended *halqah* classes, in search of that connection. At college, I joined muslim organisations in order to hear something different, which would help me make sense of my Muslim identity, my *taqwa*, my being. Honestly, I just received more Arabic and more verses which were parroted off and the translation read in English. The interpretation was just that what the reader understood it to be.

Thinking back to the work environment, I was hurt by the casual things that people would say about my faith and beliefs. It was tempting to say something in return, but I wasn't equipped. I couldn't debate because my lack of knowledge became my limitation. How could I defend my beliefs, when I couldn't understand them? I had to face people who looked at crazy things that other Muslims did and judged me accordingly.

I married into a good Muslim family. There was a repeat of the same practices. Steadfast in prayers, fasting, abstaining from all that was not proper. My husband did not have all the answers either. It seemed like we both were searching for a divine light to mysteriously appear and answer all our questions.

I still did not feel a spiritual connection; being Muslim was a sense of obligation which was directed by family, in-laws and the Muslim community. I was committed because I respected what my mother said. I practiced as any dutiful Muslim daughter, daughter-in- law and wife would, because I had a fear that if I didn't, I would be cast into hell and never forgiven. I was so afraid of a harsh *Creator.*

I think I lived in a daze for most of my early years. I was merely lost in translation.

Epiphany

> *"Grind yourself, strip yourself down to blind loving silence; stay there, until you see you are gazing at the Light with its own ageless eyes."*
> *Rumi*

The moment of epiphany came when I gave birth to my son, Ridwaan.

At twenty-one, I was responsible for this amazing gift. How would I educate him, nurture him and help him discover the jewels of our faith if I did not know them or fully understand them? I wanted him to be able to live the faith and not merely be forced into believing for the sake of it. I had to challenge what I thought was limiting my faith; I wanted to understand the foundation of my beliefs on a deeper level.

I recall having a long chat with a relative, who is a learned scholar. I expected him to judge me for being at this junction or see me as a rebellious young person. Instead he advised me that it was a process, that it involved self-discovery, and he told me meditation is a way to find wisdom.

I asked him, "Isn't meditation un-Islamic?" He laughed and said, "*Dhikr* itself is meditation. *Salaah* itself is a source of peace and contentment. Especially when done alone, in the night, for *tahajjud* prayers as was done by the Prophet Muhammad (*SAW*). Allah is not with a person if he does not want to know his *Creator* from his heart." I was amazed; I always thought meditation was *haraam* because the Buddhist /Hindus meditated. I also mentioned to him that the best part of my prayer was at the end, when I raised my hands and poured out my heart to my *Creator*. He pointed out that there was the link.

He helped me immensely, he made me realise that I should stop seeing my *deen* as two separate entities, but rather an all-encompassing part of my life; practicing doesn't only make you a Muslim, living it and believing in it wholeheartedly is what everyone should be striving for. I needed to stop worrying about how everyone saw me and start worrying about how I connected with my *Creator*.

It's amazing how one person could help me figure out the missing pieces in this wonderful puzzle!

Sometimes, being "lost" on the path is really an opening.

Journey to the centre of my world

> *"There is a candle in your heart, ready to be kindled.*
> *There is a void in your soul, ready to be filled. You feel it, don't you?"*
> *Rumi*

Thus began my journey:

- My conversations with my *Creator*.
- Reading the Quran in English, so that I could understand what I was reading.
- Researching the why's, how's, and purpose of each aspect of my faith. By the way, I am still learning every day.
- Addressing the right questions to the right people, when I didn't understand. It wasn't being blasphemous, it was seeking to understand.

Over the next few years, I was able to permeate the boundaries of myself; there was an awakening to my inner and outer worlds. It's amazing how this connection developed; it's as if someone had switched on the light within me. I just needed the guidance without being ostracised for wanting to find myself, and that for me was liberating.

My feelings, my body and my mental experiences were awakened. Once I became aware of what is going on inside my mind and body my understanding deepened and I began to articulate the essential nature and the meaning of my beliefs. I could feel this spiritual charge. When people try to describe an overwhelming experience to you, they probably end up saying, "How can I relate this experience, it's indescribable, you have to go through it to know what I mean!"

That's exactly how this happened. We all have a spiritual mirror. I felt free enough to ask myself questions like, "Who is Allah to ME?" and "What is my Muslim IDENTITY?"

One has to ask through your heart and quiet your mind to the buzz of the world. When you experience this connection, it's not some bright light or sign which we expect it to be. Rather it's the control of your mind, body and soul. Your eyes can be wide open, but it's as if you are blind. Your ears strain to hear any voice or sound, but you don't hear anything. It's almost as if you are on pause, all your thoughts sinking away. In that moment I realise where I was: I was enveloped in PEACE. I had found that inner peace, and there was solace in this quietness; a very deep Zen moment.

Who is my Creator to me?

> *"I looked in temples, churches, and mosques,*
> *but I found the Divine within my heart."*
> *Rumi*

I found Almighty to be everything: my source of life, wellbeing, joy and love. Deep inside I know that I am never separate from Allah. I kept thinking I was separate because of my sense of guilt, shame and unworthiness because I didn't feel that spiritual connection. When I came to the place in my life where I asked without shame "who is Allah?" I was able to help myself as a Muslim woman to seek the answer within me because the answers are truly within us.

I used to believe that Allah is a separate being from whom I am asking something. I found Allah is already inside me. Allah is, and always was, aligned on every level of my being. I don't have a mortal best friend in life, my best friend is my *Creator*, never failing me, always there, healing, understanding, guiding, my lighthouse on the darkest of nights. A Higher Power had taken me from where I was to where I am right now; this was done with unconditional love and patience.

Allah is peace, my inner peace, a choice seemingly made by me, but not entirely by me. Perhaps like a seed in our heart, Almighty is there waiting to be nurtured, waiting to show us our true selves, our true potential. You will not find the truth unless you are sincere. If you are not sincere, you will not get that true connection. Whether we realise it or not, we're all looking for a way to feel connected with our *Creator*. No one gave me a map on how to find my *Creator*, here Saffiya, X marks the spot. This was the biggest eye-opener for me, because I found my *Creator* in my quietest moments and when I was all alone.

This deeper love and understanding manifested when my name was called for *Hajj* in 2003, and then again for *Umrah* with my mother in 2006. These experiences were a huge turning point in my life. It just reinforced my relationship with my *Source* more and more. I had surrendered to a power greater than myself because I sure hadn't been able to help myself on my own. I just hadn't been able to believe that the shadowy aspects of me could possibly be a lesson from which I could learn.

It is written that there are 70 000 veils between us and the Almighty. We become so engrossed in our daily lives that we forget Allah. It is also written that we are forgetful creatures. As individual human beings we are given the light of Islam through the *sunnah* of our Holy Prophet (*SAW*). The choice is ours.

The starting point is when I was born and the end is with Allah. The path is every moment and every second. I wept for the time I had lost, if only I had sought the truth sooner. If only I had tried to know Allah earlier in life, instead of looking at others for answers, when the answers were within me from the very beginning.

When we enter into a conscious relationship with Allah it is both our actions, and more importantly, our intention which draws us closer to Allah. Instead of being this robotic Muslim, I wanted to feel and experience my faith, live it from deep within me. People have been searching for the Almighty for as long as we had words to describe the search. Looking for Almighty outside of yourself is like looking for your sunglasses when they are on the top of your head all along.

Most people would look at me and say, "But you are not pious, you don't dress in this manner, you work in an environment where there is inter-mingling, etc."

It took a long time to develop to get to this stage – to realise it's not about what others think or say, it's about my consciousness of my *Creator*, my actions, my words, my treatment of others; how I conduct my daily life, that is my *Taqwa*. You cannot compartmentalise Islam. You cannot isolate your faith from you. It is closer to you than your blood.

For me, being a Muslim is acknowledging *Tawheed* – the Oneness of Allah. This means I see Allah reverberate through the universe in a profound and magical way. I believe in One *Creator* as the source of a million different truths and paths, and I find *Quranic* wisdom in different places not necessarily "Muslim ones".

There was meaning to my daily prayers, there was meaning in my recitation, and there was meaning to the fasts I kept. The words I spoke had power. Every time I said or thought of something, it carried a specific vibration that either opened me up to that divine connection with Allah or caused me to contract away from the connection.

An inspirational *Sufi* tweeter said, "The *Sunnah* of Prophet Muhammad (*SAW*) demands personal authenticity as key to worship."

The emphasis is on "personal". True spirituality should empower and liberate one rather than constrict.

Previously my body showed up for prayers, but my mind was someplace else. There were times my mind showed up, but my body got left behind.

Now I am awake, all of me … mind, body and soul.

I believe

"For light I go directly to the Source of light, not to any of the reflections."
Peace Pilgrim

I believe that the power of prayer does not come from how many times we recite a prayer nor is it about just showing up for prayers five times a day. Whether you face *Makkah*, or the Wailing Wall. Whether you could sit in a church all day, light candles or ring the temple bells until your fingers bleed. The power comes from the depths of your soul and from the sincerity of your heart.

I believe that the power of prayer comes from deep within. We have been taught how to pray, supplications and recitations, whether you do it standing up or sitting with your legs tucked under you. You could have special garments which you wear for prayers. From a *burkah* to a *yarmulke*, it's from that intimate relationship one has with your *Creator*.

I believe it's OKAY to be a less-than-perfect Muslim as long as I don't harm anyone with my words or actions. I believe I need to uphold decent ethical values. I stand before my *Creator* as a work in progress and I have learnt to let go of not appearing "perfect" to the external world.

I believe I don't have to dress in the Islamic team uniform or bend to every little ruling by others for them to consider me to be an authentic Muslim.

I believe I am on a spiritual journey at my own pace and no one should judge me if I choose to stop along the way to understand why I am on this path.

I believe that being a Muslim in full essence is about compassion: compassion for the self and for all of humanity. Compassion is what makes us fully human. For me, uplifting others, being compassionate and kind, being "*soft with the world*" is my Islam. There is not a day that goes by where I do not think of Allah, even if my prayers remain unobserved. Real observance is being authentic with the world as an honour to Prophet Muhammad (*SAW*) and Allah in hopes that my own light will benefit humanity, even in the smallest of ways

I believe I am still redefining my Islam. I started at a point, just as one opens the *Quran* and recites the first *ayat*, but instead of closing the *Quran*, I am in continuous recitation mode as I am, as I said, a work in progress thus making me accessible to humanity, compassion, and kindness.

I believe that I am worthy and even in those frequent moments that I fall short of the Almighty's glory after all I am only human, and my *Creator* is forgiving.

While I may not understand every in-depth reason why certain things happen, I know what my true purpose is as a Muslim woman, to worship my *Creator* with every essence of my being. It is part of the divine plan for my life. When we approach our tests with that frame of mind, we cannot but gain from our experience, *Insha'Allah.*

> *"You are a volume in the divine book*
> *A mirror to the power that created the universe*
> *Whatever you want, ask it of yourself*
> *Whatever you're looking for can only be found*
> *Inside of you."*
> *Rumi, The Rubais of Rumi: Insane with Love*

May Allah guides us all to the straight path, *Aameen.*

PART THREE

Marriage and beyond

The tale of two sorrows

Zakiyyah Asmall

My story begins on the day I got married to the love of my life – thirteen May 2007, a day before my twenty-second birthday. I was a funky adolescent back then, with a bizarre zest for life – an accountant in the making, an artist at heart, and a poet to some. My groom, elegantly clad in a deep chocolate-brown suit, was 1.8 metres tall, well built, twenty-seven years old, a B.Com Honours graduate, CFO for the Public Protector and an ex-rugby player. I still recall every unique detail of that magical day, from the sweetness of his smile to the classy bronze and gold decor combined with delicate baby pink and pale cream roses. Set against the perfect backdrop of lush greenery and breathtaking mountainous scenery, the day I married Zainul Aberdeen was all too perfect.

Our hours and days passed in pure bliss and sweet romantic interludes. Every corner of our two-bedroom, upmarket apartment in the heart of Johannesburg's northern suburbs echoed with the sweet sounds of laughter and blissful sentiments. I took the role of diligent housewife, simultaneously pursuing my studies through correspondence, and spent the evenings waiting in anticipation for my husband's return. Zain – as untidy and disorganised as he was – had the profound traits of wisdom, calmness and maturity. He thoroughly enjoyed the challenging and intricate nature of his profession, travelling daily to the heart of Pretoria's CBD where his office was based.

My home was my palace, filled with jewels of eternal memories and enchanted moments. With Zain as my prince, I felt like a princess in the true sense of the word. At first my days revolved around preparing scrumptious meals, experimenting with exotic dishes and trying my utmost to be a perfect housewife to the one who truly deserved the best. Soon enough, however, my household chores started to become monotonous and my career-oriented mind craved stimulation. To help me on the pathway to becoming a successful chartered accountant, I found a post at an accounting firm. Being a quiet, simple Muslim girl who prayed *salaah* regularly, I was anxious about leaving my sheltered environment to face the workplace alone. Zain, my pillar of strength, was there all the way, reassuring me with love and understanding. He allowed me the opportunity to step into the corporate world and become an independent, strong individual with new-found abilities and potentials.

I was mesmerised, enchanted and dazzled – more than words could ever express. It was our first anniversary and I had been whisked off to a secluded restaurant and showered with gifts and a card which read, "Here's to 70 more." The entrance of the restaurant boasted a unique water feature, which flowed down the stairway into the dining area, where crystal chandeliers hung low, adding a perfect charm to the romantic atmosphere. The next day was my twenty-third birthday. A bunch of red roses awaited me with another card that read, "Will you be my sweetheart forever?" The words on these cards, carefully chosen and written with hope and love still ring in my ears and create confusion in my mind, causing me to shed tears and to pray to Almighty Allah.

It was the last few days of the blessed month of *Ramadan*, the Islamic year of 1428. Zain had flown to France with the Public Protector, his first trip out of South Africa. He was anxious about leaving me, but I reassured him that I would be more than okay, even though I was deeply saddened by his departure and about spending *Eid-ul-Fitr* away from him. But he did not give me much of an opportunity to miss him, for he called daily all the way from the city of lights and love – Paris. During the time that he was away, I enjoyed the calmness and serenity of my home town, as I was preparing to write my examination. His absence left a longing in my heart and I felt a deep-rooted sense of appreciation for him. My arms ached to reach out to him and show him, with love and compassion, just how grateful I was that he was a part of my life. The day he landed at Oliver Tambo International Airport, feelings of relief and excitement washed over me. I couldn't wait to see him. He assured me that he was going to drive up to Newcastle the very next day just to spend time with me and his parents in Glencoe.

The fifth of October 2008 was a cold, gloomy day; all too depressing and dreary, as grey clouds covered the sky and a soft drizzle fell to the ground, causing the spring air to smell dense with the first summer rains. I was studying to write an accounting examination the next day but restless and uneasy feelings crept over me, causing my tears to flow profusely. Anxious, uncertain, and overwhelming emotions took over my senses and the gloom set in. Was it due to the dreariness of the dull day or due to another unknown and unforeseen reason? I had spent the entire morning in wasted anticipation, awaiting Zain's arrival, but he had driven to his parents' home instead. "I don't want to disturb you," he said, "I want you to study." I was upset and had cut the call in a regrettable fit of rage. My mum, seeing me in my perturbed state asked, "What would you do if something had to happen to him?" I bluntly said, "I wouldn't be able to live without him." If only I had known the serious nature of my words and understood their importance in the plan that Allah had for me. If only I had been wiser, and had realised that every moment and every event in my life was already predestined. If only I had taken time to perfect my beautiful *deen*, then maybe, just maybe I would have been better prepared for the events that were about to unfold.

The day slowly turned into night, bringing with it an eeriness that engulfed the chilly air and grasped the starlit sky in its icy grip. Zain had spent the day with his parents and was on his way back to Johannesburg, with his sister and friend to accompany him. It was at eight that evening when I heard his car at the main gate. My mum came into my room, where I was aimlessly trying to study. All she said was, "Please just talk to him." I heard him at the kitchen door and the sound of his deep voice sent waves of ecstasy running down my spine, causing my heart to beat faster and my pulse to quicken. He entered my room and said to me, "Please look at me." My eyes were filled with tears and my heart with some unknown anxiety and I didn't want him to see it all. I turned around and there he was, an angel; my Allah had blessed me with more than I could have asked for. His fair skin glowed, his dark hair curly as always and his smile – just perfect. He spoke to me softly, kissing my tears with his rosy lips. He told me how much he missed me, how beautiful I am and that I should never cry. He spoke of spending time with me when my exams were over, of never leaving me again. I smiled and my soul felt alive and whole again. He embraced me, tightly. As I walked him to the car, I begged him to stay the night, but to no avail. He kissed my forehead and cheeks and I laughed at him. "What's wrong with you?" I said. I watched him leave with a heavy heart, but with hope and love and faith that we had a future ahead, to grow, to learn, to connect with each other and form a unique, everlasting bond.

The call came at around eleven that night, when my mum, my sister and I were snuggled up in bed, having a good chat. My dad walked into the room and broke the news to us. There had been an accident, but my dad assured us that they were no casualties. My heart plummeted, my throat was constricted and my mind raced with unpleasant thoughts. My dad rushed to the accident scene, leaving us to dwell on our anxieties. I prayed, performed two *rakaats* of *salaah* with sincerity, devotion and appreciation. Time ticked away, it was approximately 12.30 a.m. when the phone rang, piercing the quiet hallway with its shrieking tone. On that chilly October night I listened to the conversation between my parents and the words hit me with a blow to my stomach. "Zain's gone," my mum kept repeating. I was inconsolable, calling his name and refusing to accept the inevitable. I remember that people came, crowding around me, and the sound of their sympathetic voices, but most of all I remember the pain, the uncontrollable, lingering pain.

"To Allah do we belong and to him is our return." These words I unconsciously repeated as we made our way towards Glencoe. My eyes felt heavy and dark circles outlined them due to excessive crying and lack of sleep. The journey was slow and agonising. I remember the events as they unfolded; they remain imprinted on my mind, still fresh and raw. I remember sitting next to his lifeless being and refusing to touch him. I kept saying to myself, "This is not my Zain." He was warm, vibrant and energetic just a few hours ago. I remember his mom stroking his hair gently and saying, "Zain wake up, my son wake up." I remember feeling his cold, cold cheek against my skin. I remember staring at his flawless and beautiful face and weeping. I remember making a silent *duah* for him, "Oh, Allah, he was so good to me, so please my Lord grant him the highest stages and forgive him for his shortcomings." I remember the verses of the *Quran* being recited and family sobbing, some gasping, some uncontrollable. I remember watching with helpless eyes as the menfolk came and then he was gone, taken to his eternal abode with only his deeds to accompany him.

The four months and ten days that I spent within the confines of my parents' home were unbearable. I prayed excessively during this time. I prayed for courage and strength, for ease, for wisdom and understanding. The evenings were the most difficult. Lonely and unpleasant feelings would haunt me and the pain was like a knife through my heart. My work colleagues paid me a surprise visit and were sympathetic and reassuring. I had been granted leave from work but I kept my mind occupied with hobbies so the thoughts could fade away for a while. I had postponed my examination till a later stage when I was ready to pursue my career once again. Two weeks after the tragedy I made my way to the "city of gold" – Johannesburg – accompanied by my parents and his as well. We had to undertake the tedious and heart-breaking task of clearing out our belongings from our apartment as the rental was accumulating. I entered the apartment and was greeted by Zain's untidy clutter of dirty dishes, sweet wrappers, an unmade bed and clothes galore. What in the past would have been a reason to shout at him was now the reason for my tears to flow. I wept out of love, out of despair, out of anguish and rage. I wept bitterly as I packed my sweetheart's belongings into a small cardboard box, sealed it with a sore heart and marked it with his name. I stood for a while pondering over the little that he owned, the deeds that accompanied him and the sheets that he was enshrouded in. The reality then dawned on me that this life is a phase and it was about time I awoke from my slumber and began to strive for the hereafter.

At the end of my mourning period, I gained the courage and inner strength to attempt taking on the big city life alone. I was determined and inspired to make a fresh start and achieve my goals. Eight months later, feelings of unworthiness and extreme loneliness caused me to leave the city and to reside in Newcastle once again.

Being an unmarried, widowed girl amongst the Indian community I experienced feelings of inferiority, low self-esteem and harsh comments that caused me to feel a desperate need to remarry. In February 2010, I received my first proposal. I was sceptical and unsure at first but community and family members felt the need to convince me otherwise. I performed *istikharah salaah* but I still remained quite uncertain. Feelings of inadequacy haunted my thoughts and overpowered my ability to think reasonably and clearly. I felt as if being single was some sort of curse or tragic event that I had brought upon myself. Eventually, after two weeks of *duah*, tears and contemplation I agreed. I was given three months, after pleading for time, to write my examination and prepare myself for marriage. I was rushed into setting a date and mentally pumping myself up for the commitment of a lifetime. I was soon to be married into a foreign family, to an unknown person who I was told was a "good boy". From what I assessed of him, he was quiet, reserved, orthodox and old-fashioned. Chats on Facebook and Mxit were a big no-no. I did not want to have kids for at least a year into the marriage but he did not believe in contraception and made it clear that it was against his religious beliefs and he wasn't willing to compromise on the issue. Although it was clear I was going to have to make sacrifices in many aspects of my life, I still chose to enter into the sacred bond of marriage, willing to accept and hoping that love would somehow develop and conquer all.

I was married on 13 June 2010, in a beautiful garden where palm trees stood tall and a deep blue pool glistened, adding the perfect touch to the serene ambience. I wore a dusty pink and peach beaded raw silk gown with a matching chiffon scarf and gold accessories. The wedding function was small and private, with just a few close family and friends. I experienced all sorts of emotions that twisted my insides into knots of fears and anxieties. My new home was situated on the South Coast, approximately four hundred kilometres from my home town and was the small back section to his parents' residence. The first few months were the worst as I felt trapped, depressed and alone. I soon adjusted to my surroundings but was accused and belittled at times. I felt incapable and unworthy. I did not tell anyone of my sorrows during these times and I tried my utmost to be the perfect wife but I always felt like I was lacking in my duties. I was forced into becoming entirely dependent on him for my every need as I was not allowed to leave the house on my own or with friends. I craved freedom in the sense of being able to perform simple tasks on my own or just being able to attend religious classes weekly. There were times when I wept bitterly, not knowing what action of mine could have caused my husband not to speak to me. Soon my ties with my mum were weakened, as I was told that I should not speak to her daily. I was made to believe that she was controlling our lives and this was upsetting him – I should not listen to her advice but to him instead. I had reached a point of complete submission and total control of my life was given to this man. I chose to remain silent through it all.

I fell pregnant during the second month of marriage and, despite my feelings about the marriage, I was ecstatic. Maryam was born on 10 April 2011 by C-section, a perfect weight of 2.7 kilograms. My parents were there, proud and joyous, but soon things went from bad to worse. My baby had been born with an eye infection and became dehydrated due to her inadequate feeding and lack of the required medical care.

Eventually my mum forced the issue and Maryam had to be hospitalised. I felt like my world was falling apart and my in-laws were not making it any easier. All sorts of accusations were made to my parents and nasty comments were made. Once I had gone to my parents' home for some rest, I felt relieved to a certain extent. I had time to ponder over my marriage and I confided in my mum, as I had always been close to her. In the end, I didn't go back to my husband and I was separated for ten months. There were endless arguments and attempts to reconcile but to no avail. I was not willing to return under the same conditions and I was unhappy in the marriage. We were divorced thereafter.

Today Maryam is a year and two months old. She has been my reason to live since the day she was born. I don't regret the second marriage as without it I wouldn't have had her and I wouldn't have learnt life's great lessons of patience, self-sacrifice and courage. I am currently striving to complete the last few modules towards my degree and hope to rejoin the corporate world soon. I believe everything happens for a reason and only Allah knows the wisdom behind those reasons. This, therefore, is the tale of my two sorrows – my journey of life, love and destiny.

The road to the kitchen less travelled

Somayya Hansrod

I stood outside my in-laws' house, rang the doorbell, and nervously waited alongside my husband. For the umpteenth time that day, I pleaded with him to eat my dessert and pretend that he enjoyed it, even if he did not. Aadil was not too impressed but nonetheless I bargained with him. I promised that if he played his part this "last" time I would not demand that he take me to my mother's house. Aadil once more reminded me that if I followed the recipe, then everything would be perfect.

Aadil is very familiar with my antics in the kitchen, which include innovating and adjusting recipes. I remember the time when I cooked the butter chicken without any butter and when the *falooda* dessert became *falooda* milkshake because I only used half the required quantity of *ghas* powder. Aadil has renamed the chicken casserole that I make "casserole a la leftovers", because it consists of a fine blend of all the foods we enjoyed during the week.

I am not a typical Muslim, Indian wife. I can't make a decent shaped *roti*; my children have never tasted *mugh dhal, channa dhal* or *vengra*. My *tarkari* comes in two varieties, either the soup version, which generally occurs when I decide to have a nap while the curry is cooking and add extra water so that it doesn't burn before I wake up; or the UV version which is when the colour of my curry is so bright that you are likely to develop a tan just by looking at it. The curry becomes a deep red colour when I try to balance the *garam masala* that I have added with large quantities of tomato puree. Aadil often expresses thanks that my mother lives close to us and he lovingly wonders why the apple fell so far from the tree.

A Muslim Indian woman's culinary skill is crucial when establishing her worth as marriage material. Fortunately for me, my husband is not particular or fussy about what I place before him at supper time. In my house, my family has two choices: they can either eat what's on offer (however unappetising it might look) or they can mix a bowl of cereal. It is a well-known fact that breakfast is the most important meal of the day and, fortunately for my family, there are days when they can enjoy breakfast three times a day.

Nanima is never pleased when she coincidentally phones at supper time and her favourite grandson tells her that he is having Weet-Bix for supper. In my defence, I often argue that Weet-Bix has far greater nutritional content and is far better than oily, rich mutton *tarkari.* I am convinced that Weet-Bix would actually give my family a longer and healthier life expectancy. Aadil disagrees and argues that he would prefer to die earlier with *ghee* soaked *roti* in his stomach than later with a Weet-Bix overdose.

When I married, I bought every recipe book and tried every dish because I wanted to please and impress my darling husband. However, my enthusiasm in the kitchen was short lived, and two years later, with the arrival of my firstborn, my daughter Naailah, everything changed. As my husband puts it, "When my wife and firstborn arrived from the hospital, many other things arrived with them as well, like frozen meals, a reduction of daily meals, the introduction of a staple side dish – frozen, ready cut chips – and, the cherry on top: toasted cheese, toasted cheese and more toasted cheese." A further two pregnancies later, coupled with a teaching job, saw a drastic reduction in the time I spent in the kitchen. I only managed to make dessert for *Eid.* I cooked meals which required *vagaar* on Fridays only and meals which included variety were left to be enjoyed at *Nanima's* house. Baked chicken, grilled chicken, chicken casserole and chicken strips became the standard weekly menu.

Generally, I can prepare a traditional Indian meal with the help of the numerous recipe books that are available. However, making the *biryani* just the way my mother-in-law makes it or getting the texture of the *burfee* to be as perfect as my grandmother-in-law's, makes time spent in the kitchen very traumatic, so that preparing a tin of baked beans has become rocket science.

My "porridge brain" which has become permanent after having three children makes me forget to attend cooking classes or I forget what I learnt at the class, or I mix up the directions to the venue and land up at the book store instead! Consequently, when I should have been mastering the art of creating the perfect pot of *biryani,* I was engrossed in *Mornings in Jenin.* When I could have acquired the skill for the creamiest *burfee*, I was occupied with *The Kite Runner*. When I should have been perfecting the fine motor skills required for folding the perfect *samoosa*, I was mesmerised by *The Power of One*. A lesson in biscuit making was swapped for the intrigue and suspense of *Snow Child*. And when all the ladies in Roshnee were competing in the annual pre-*Ramadaan* savoury challenge, I was engrossed in the gripping *Hunger Games*.

After frequently hearing that her grandchildren had toasted cheese for supper or that her son-in-law had nutella on bread for lunch, my dear mother began preparing frozen meals (which my family refers to as "freezies") for me to defrost and cook. My husband and children were overjoyed with the arrival of *Nani's* freezies because they finally got to enjoy meals like *aaloobedda*, *kalya*, green beans *tarkari* and fish *biryani* as well as extras like *roti*, *puri* and *katchoomer*. Everyone was happy and I was over the moon because my time spent in the kitchen was generously reduced. I could spend more time doing my three most enjoyable hobbies – reading, writing and enjoying a good cup of tea with homemade biscuits.

However, with the introduction of *Nani's* freezies I felt as though I was no longer appreciated by my husband and children. When I made an attempt to cook, my cooking was always compared to my mother's. It hurt to hear my four-year-old exclaim that *Nani's* viennas were "fried" better than mine. To add insult to injury, my husband would say at the end of each meal, "Please phone *Nanima* and tell her the meal was lovely!" I often asked myself, doesn't defrosting a meal, placing it in a correctly sized pot, allowing it to cook at the appropriate heat, ensuring it doesn't burn and finally placing the pot on the table, count for something?

After much humiliation, embarrassment and being on the receiving end of far too many burnt-cooking jokes, I have accepted that I will never be able to cook like *Nanima*. So, to ensure that my family live longer, I have taken heed of the words of wisdom I once read, "Approach cooking with reckless abandon!" Since I am already reckless in the kitchen, I have decided to abandon cooking completely.

There are advantages to my disinterest in cooking – my sons may not demand or even expect elaborate and lavish meals from their wives and my husband may not suffer from cholesterol or heart disease later in life. The problem, however, is that my daughter is learning my bad cooking habits. My prayer for my dear daughter is that Allah grants her a husband who is a chef, *Aameen.*

Being a proud Muslim woman, my story would not be complete without offering the customary recipe or two. So I end with three recipes which I have mastered and which have been my lifeline on numerous occasions:

Pasta in a rush

Ingredients: spaghetti (cooked), 3 spices (Aromat, mixed herbs and Spice For Rice), 3 peppers (green, red, yellow), 1 tub fresh cream and 1 tub sour cream

Method: Braise peppers in spices and add spaghetti. Lastly add one tub fresh cream and one tub sour cream. (You can omit either of the creams without serious consequences).

Somayya's standard sweet treat

Ingredients: baked tarts, caramel, Nestlé cream, bananas

Method: Spread caramel on baked tarts, layer bananas on top, cover with Nestlé cream. If you are taking the treat to your in-laws, you can decorate with Nestlé chocolate flake. And in case you are wondering, *Nanima* sends me the ready cut tarts; I just bake them.

Lemon punch for unexpected guests

(Perfect for when the only thing you have to offer is water and you can't make tea because you don't have biscuits to serve with it)

Ingredients: 1 peeled lemon, 1 cup sugar, 4 cups water

Method: Liquidise for only a few seconds, strain and serve. Thereafter, walk tall, smile and be engulfed by the flood of compliments.

MahabbaLillah, my child

Adeela Kasoojee

Today I read a blog post that took me back four years to the night that you were born – a cold night in July. The lady that penned it encouraged mothers to love their children for the sake of Allah alone – *MahabbaLillah*. So often have I reminded myself to do the same. But, is it possible for a mother to love a child for the sake of her *Rabb* alone?

If you had asked me this question several years ago, I would have answered with a resounding "yes" and argued that it was wholly possible. I wasn't a mother, you see. I wasn't even a wife. I was a young woman finding her forte; navigating through this maze we call "life". Having just lost my dearly loved father at that time, I kept reminding myself that perhaps it was not wise to experience love, that to love was to expose oneself to the possibility of heartbreak and pain. After the loss of my daddy, I wasn't ready to let someone into my life and then risk losing them later on. But then I met and fell in love with your father. Allah is the best of planners. What I had planned and what He intended were two different paths. His will prevailed and I knew love despite my aversion to it. I learnt that the human spirit is resilient and can be mended when it is broken; and your daddy was the balm that helped in mending mine.

The question about a mother's love crossed my mind when I found out that you were on your way. I had wanted a baby for so long, you see. All the insecurities and doubts that I ever had were trebled and I kept thinking about whether I deserved this awesome opportunity and beautiful responsibility.

The night you were born, you seemed so different from the busy little being that had occupied my body and thoughts for nine months. I could not have imagined the type of a person you would turn out to be once you were here or what you would look like. All I knew, before you made your way into my world, is that I somehow believed that raising a son would have been a far easier option. After all, I was still having difficulty with being a daughter to a mother, and I thought, from my limited exposure to the relationships between mothers and their female children, that the last thing I needed was to be a mother to a daughter. Your daddy, on the other hand, was convinced that you were a gorgeous little girl but refused to allow me to have a 4D ultrasound scan. Looking back, I'm glad that he refused. I grappled with this issue about your sex for my entire pregnancy, wondering and dreaming; happy, but also afraid. The Almighty, however, in His infinite wisdom sent me a little girl to love and cherish.

After your birth, fresh from the warm confines of my womb, you lay sleeping peacefully in your little glass bassinet like a living doll. Porcelain-tinged with a pink glow, you made little mewling noises like a newly born kitten when you were hungry, your eyes closed and limbs stretching and flexing now that you were freed of your safe, warm cocoon.

I was a mess. I could hardly sleep in the days that followed, for the fear and doubts that swamped me. My ineptitude encircled me like a vice-grip. Burgeoning doubts ate away at my joy of your birth and I questioned my motives. Suddenly your gender was not an issue. What selfish, irresponsible thing had I done by bringing another human into a cruel callous world? How was I going to cope with a baby? How presumptuous and arrogant of me to assume that I, in all my selfishness, could care for another being and be at the beck and call of a child, responsible for her every need, charged with her care and upbringing. With my lack of parenting skills and the huge financial implications of raising a child, how was I going to keep you alive and well?

All of these doubts ate away at me, reducing me to a noisy, frightened mess of tears. I became convinced of my inability to nurture you so that you would thrive. I was a maelstrom of emotions and excitement, despite my textbook preparation. Here I was faced with a real, living, breathing baby and she was not textbook and neither were my reactions. At home, it was worse. Everyone wanted to be your mother and I felt ineffectual and awkwardly jealous. Their practiced hands made me seem clumsy and without purpose and I wondered if we would ever fit together – you and me; like the pieces in a mother–child puzzle.

I chose to breastfeed you, watching your warm, fuzzy little head nuzzle into my breast and seek out the life-giving nectar that my body produced for you alone, forcing myself to endure the painful sucking, despite everyone's objections that you were hungry and the notion that I had no milk.

My persistence paid off.

It was amazing that this simple act of breastfeeding became so comfortable and natural in the months that followed. You and I had finally found each other. The frequent stops you would make whilst feeding, to gaze into my eyes with love and trust and then break into a dazzling smile, tugged at my heartstrings and opened the portal into the unknown. I found myself loving with the wild abandon that only a mother can muster.

It is not unusual that the maternal bond is not always immediate. It is developed over time with patience and space. People fail to realise that a new mother needs to spend time with her little baby in order for her to be able to love later, with the intensity that she does. It's falling in love, not love at first sight: a gradual journey that requires much sacrifice and understanding. Social media and literature tend to romanticise the relationship, never acknowledging how much time and effort it takes for two strangers to "fall in love".

You and I were strangers that fell in love. But, oh, what love!

Hey, don't get me wrong, it's not all sunshine and roses. We've had our bad days. A little girl aching to explore and learn sometimes has a mother afraid to let her spread her wings and possibly experience pain and disappointment.

I don't consider myself to be particularly maternal. I lack the patience and easy candour that makes certain people "ideal parent material" but when it comes to you, am different.

I would commit heinous crimes if anyone thought to hurt you. I ache for you when you sob at some imagined injustice, and, when you shriek that you "hate" me in the heat of a tantrum, my heart lurches. I know that you do not mean it because five minutes later you profess undying love. Nonetheless, the mere thought that you could hate me is so disturbing that it creates a dull, physical pain in my chest. My bond with my own mother was not as free and I don't recall her being as central to my life as I am to yours. Perhaps she was, but I can't remember much of it. We lived in a different time, when children were "seen and not heard". To speak our minds when we were as little as you are now was to risk being rebuked. You, on the other hand are both seen and heard – vocal, loud and opinionated. I wouldn't have it any other way.

My relationship with my mother has changed now and I believe that I owe much of it to you. You made me see myself for who I am and my own mother for who she is – simply human. No airs and graces and higher sentient beings here; merely human beings with all the faults and foibles, love and care, insecurities and uncertainties of our species and also inherited traits, both good and bad, whether we like it or not.

Inherited traits …

When I look at you, with your easy disposition and sunny smiles, I see much of both myself and your beloved father. Yes, your sunny smile, temper tantrums and abundant way with words are my traits; and your need for personal time, your small kindnesses towards everyone around you and beautiful pouting lips when you are sad or when you don't get your way are a replica of your daddy.

Yet your father and I also see you as your own person, with your own hopes and dreams. Not an extension of me or him and certainly not a clone. You are unique and he always reminds me of that. No one will ever be exactly like you in this world. You are our child, born and raised in love.

Khalil Gibran says it beautifully in *The Prophet*:

And a woman who held a babe against her bosom said, "Speak to us of Children".
And he said:
Your children are not your children.
They are the sons and daughters of Life's longing for itself.
They come through you but not from you,
And though they are with you, yet they belong not to you.
You may give them your love but not your thoughts.
For they have their own thoughts.
You may house their bodies but not their souls,

For their souls dwell in the house of tomorrow, which you cannot visit, not even in your dreams.
You may strive to be like them, but seek not to make them like you.
For life goes not backward nor tarries with yesterday.

You are you. Not me. You will never be me and I will never be you. But that's okay. You will forge your own dreams and carve your own path through life as I have done. I will support your choices and decisions even if I have no love for them because that is my job as your mother: to love you for who you are, without qualification or expectations or limitations, to love you with all the love that a mother can muster, with strength in adversity and calm in the storm of your life.

I have tried to love you only for the sake of Allah but I have failed. Allah is the Almighty, Omniscient in His power and infinite in capacity. So *MahabbaLillah*, my child – I love you for the sake of Allah and beyond that; for the capacity that He created within my soul to love with wild abandon as only a mother can. He is your *Creator* and mine – never forget that and know always to live your life in fulfillment, without regret or denial except that which is forbidden to you. *Insha'Allah Aameen*!

To Mummy, with love

Shireen Sabodien

Before marriage

Ah, the spoilt little mummy's girl, always being favoured by Mummy – and Daddy, of course. Why is that, you asked? I was the baby and only daughter, that's why, and it was lovely to have two older brothers. I "got away with murder" as the saying goes.

Mummy was a hard working woman. She earned so little for the time and effort she spent and yet she was satisfied. Mummy allowed me freedom, whereas Daddy was super strict and always said "NO". Mummy said, "Just look after yourself and don't be so loud." Oh, Mummy, do you know that I'm just like you?

It always amazed me that Mummy was a good Muslim. She converted many years ago and all my friends thought she was born a Muslim. She didn't allow me to leave the house without a scarf. I called her the "*doekie* police". My headscarf became my identity. My non-Muslim friends said I looked weird without a headscarf if I took it off wanting to fit in or look cool with them. I came to love wearing my headscarf. I hate it when my ears are uncovered. Mummy, you taught me well, *shukran*.

I loved reading and I did well at school. Mummy was naughty – she introduced me to "Mills & Boon". After finishing school, Mummy insisted that I study further as she wanted me to have more in life than she had. She wanted me to be a financially independent woman and not dependent on a man. In hindsight, my mummy was clever.

Alhamdulillah, I graduated with an information technology degree and immediately got a job offer from Caltex Oil (Chevron South Africa). The day I called Mummy to share the good news, she was so proud and asked, "So at which petrol station you gonna work?" Mummy is too adorable. "No, Mummy, I'm going to work at the Head Office in Cape Town as a card specialist."

In this time I met my beloved husband. Oh my, it was definitely not "love at first sight". Only after five years of friendship did I realise what a loving, committed, reliable, funny, witty "friend" I had. We married on 26 September 1999.

When married and beyond

Married life was more fulfilling than I'd imagined; having my best friend as my husband, doting parents and protective brothers. We were so happy. We were financially stable. My in-laws also helped us along. My husband has amazing parents; they are blessed people and I thank them often for the wonderful son they raised. Life could not have been better, even if I had written the script myself.

We had two lovely, chubby-cheeked little boys – Baizeed and Ijaaz – the other loves of my life. Having my own family seemed so easy. My husband helped me with everything, from raising the kids to cooking, cleaning and doing the washing. Hubby did most of the chores but that's because I was the career woman with a "title". I tell you, having money and titles can go to your head.

My husband always made me feel absolutely gorgeous. He was always kissing my feet or smelling my clothes when I was away at work because he missed me so much. He told me every day how blessed he was to have me and that he could never love anyone as much. He gave me so much love and respect and he built my confidence. We spent all our time together and being away from him was a nightmare. Mummy always said we were inseparable.

The day my world came crashing down

Friday 13 March 2009. Igshaan Sabodien declared dead at eight p.m. at age thirty-six. Head-on collision. All the bones in his body were broken. Just like me. Broken beyond words.

In a blink of an eye, I became a single parent. I became both a mother and a father to my four- and seven-year-old boys. At the age of thirty-five I became a WIDOW.

I just wanted my parents and my brothers. Mummy was my rock and my coping mechanism. She cried so much at the *janaaza*. She cried for "her" child. She wanted to see "her" child one more time. I had to console and comfort her.

As the days and months went by, Mummy taught me to live again. She took care of my babies while I dragged myself to work. I had to work, because how else would I survive? I called Mummy every day from work, asking her, "What's for supper?" We would speak for a long time. She always made my favourite dish.

Then Mummy fell ill. Nothing serious, we thought. The doctors called us all in. They could do nothing more for Mummy. It couldn't be! Not MY Mummy! I just lost my husband a few months ago; not my Mummy too.

She passed away quickly, aged sixty-two. I still think it's young. So now I'm a widow and taking care of my dad who is a widower, too. He cried so much for Mummy. I knew his pain but I didn't know how to console him. I was still dealing with my own loss. The day of the *janaaza* is still a blur. I was numb, not comprehending, sad beyond words.

I lost my two pillars of strength in a short period of time. Was I going to survive this?

Another loss: in October 2010, after fourteen years at Caltex Oil, I received my retrenchment letter. I was officially unemployed. Initial sadness was replaced by relief, and the day I left my office building I couldn't have been happier.

I could take care of my children now. Daddy tried his best, but what does an almost seventy-year-old know about raising two small boys? With both Mummy and husband gone, life was challenging. I started to see and believe that the Almighty had a plan; a plan that was so much better than I could have dreamt of.

At present

It's been close to two years that I have been at home. The boys absolutely love it that I wake them up with kisses, dress them in the mornings, drop them at school and fetch them again. I love being their mother and I love the place I am in right now.

Today, I don't have the luxuries I had back then. I don't drive fancy cars anymore. I can't shop without counting my pennies – every R10 or R20 is turned over twice.

Shukr to Allah for all His mercies. I am a better person for having gone through all my trials. More importantly, I am a better Muslim. Today I turn to Allah for everything and anything as I did not have that relationship before. My conversations happen on the *musalla*, in the car and on the train. Whatever I do, I ask Allah for His mercy and guidance. Don't get me wrong; I am far from perfect. I am still a work in progress and I am trying. Yes, I truly am.

Out of the fish tank … and into the pond

Nadia Cassim

I held on tightly to the bouquet, glancing momentarily at the pink plastic pearls that the florist had glued to the roses, to make sure that they were still in place before taking my first step down the aisle. I could feel the eyes of everyone in the room on me. The first table that I passed was seated with turbaned men wearing white *kurtas* and sporting long, unkempt beards. They were staring at me too, just like the others. Strange, I thought – these were the same men who gave lectures at the mosque, telling young boys to lower their gazes when they saw women.

My thoughts were in a muddle and my palms were sweaty. I could feel the bouquet sliding down in my hands as I took the final turn towards my husband, Zain. He looked handsome in the cream and white suit and tie that his mother, Razia, had picked out for him at Cresta shopping centre two weeks previously. After three months of endless preparations and headaches, we were finally going to be married. It felt surreal.

When I drew near, Zain extended his hand for me to take and I let the bouquet slip into my left hand as my right hand reached out to touch his. I felt a tingling sensation vibrate through my body as my skin touched his. That was the first time we had touched in the eyes of Allah.

"You look beautiful," Zain whispered softly as we stepped, hand-in-hand, onto the elaborately decorated stage that Razia had so carefully designed with the wedding planner. Zain's family had paid for everything: the dress, the house and the wedding. I had tried to insist that we just perform the vows and have a small intimate gathering at home but Razia had refused. She had made sure that a formal wedding was planned. Her youngest son, her baby, deserved the best.

On the stage, two thrones stood side by side. The wedding planner ushered me to the one on the right but first I had to pose, standing with my arms leaning against the backrest, so that the photographer could take a "shot". Zain's family took turns to come up and greet me. First were his mother, Razia, and his father, Hamid, followed by his younger sister, Shaaista, and finally his brother, Yaseen, with his elegant wife, Hawa Bibi, on his arm. They each wished us good health, a blessed marriage and many children before taking their seats at the main table.

The guests no longer stared at me. Their attention was now on the platters of food that waiters in black tuxedos brought from the kitchen. My mother-in-law had catered lavishly for the three hundred guests, sparing no cost. I could see their eyes widening when they saw the seafood platters, decked with large lobsters, freshly cooked crabs and king-size prawns, on leaves of lettuce and beds of spicy rice.

Zain dug hungrily into a lobster and I nibbled on some rice and prawns. Seafood was not my favourite dish and besides, I could hardly face eating, with all the butterflies that were fluttering around in my belly. I remember thinking that I was celebrating my last hours as a virgin and feeling petrified of what was to come. I hoped that Zain would be too exhausted from all the feasting to want to "do it".

My mother-in-law had also outdone herself with the dessert menu: lemon cheesecake with strawberries and cream. I usually love to indulge in anything sweet, but I couldn't bring myself to eat. I kept glancing at the clock at the back of the hall. It was already after 12 p.m. and the guests had started to leave.

The photographer, a thin, dark-skinned woman with frizzy black hair and a scarf half-heartedly tied around her head, instructed the remaining guests to come up on stage in groups of twenty if they wanted to be in the album. By the end of the family photo shoot, my mouth ached from having to keep on smiling. If I didn't smile, the photographer just stopped the proceedings and reminded me to look happy, as it was my wedding day.

Just when my legs were beginning to cramp from all the standing, the photo shoot finally came to an end, and Zain announced that it was time for us to go. We had decided not to spend our first night together at a hotel, but in the privacy of our recently purchased flat on Church Street. We were driven home in style in the Jaguar Zain's father had hired for the night. However, a few women, who had also been at the reception, arrived at the flat before us, and were snooping around the bedroom and sprinkling rose petals all over the floor in preparation for our romantic evening together. Apparently my mother-in-law has a spare key to use in case of an emergency, and this occasion counted as one. I felt like my privacy had been invaded and that everyone would now have a mental picture of where I would be "deflowered". I was anxious and nervous and I remember thinking that perhaps going to a hotel would have been a better idea. They all finally left at two a.m. and my sister-in-law, Shaaista, who was the last to leave, winked at Zain before closing the door.

Zain turned to look at me – he was calm and in control.

"I think I'm going to wash up and get out of this wedding dress," I managed to whisper.

"Do you need some help with the zip?" he asked with a mischievous grin on his face.

I blushed.

"No, I'm fine. I'll manage by myself. Thank you." I replied a bit too formally.

I grabbed my vanity case, rushed into the bathroom and locked the door. There was a giant mirror hanging over the basin and I stared at myself for a few minutes, before making any attempt to wash off the overdone makeup and glitter that the makeup artist had spent two hours applying to my face. I slipped on my nightdress – a modest, sleeveless white silk dress cut short at the knee, revealing just a little cleavage.

Zain knocked at the door. "Is everything ok, Nadia? You've been in there for over half an hour." I was shocked that the time had melted by so quickly.

"I'm almost done," I cleared my throat. "Be out in a minute."

I took a deep breath and quickly tidied up my things which were scattered all over the place. I opened the door to find Zain lying spread out on the white duvet cover. I wanted to turn away and lock myself back in the bathroom. Although my heart began beating wildly, I mustered all the courage I possessed and climbed into the bed next to him.

"Wow," he whispered in a sexy tone. I closed my eyes.

"Now this may be a little painful," he warned.

I have promised myself never to forget that moment. It felt like a bolt of lightning had struck my entire body, leaving me wriggling in pain and numb to my toes. There was none of the sensual emotion so beautifully described in romance novels – just pain.

The day after the wedding was the *walimah*, a traditional Islamic feast hosted by the groom's side to officially welcome the bride into the family. I have never really liked the idea of a *walimah* – it makes me wonder what the guests might be thinking of the bride and what she may have been doing the night before, in her new role as "wife". When I pictured the *walimah* that morning, I felt as though everybody would stare openly at an imaginary sign pasted to me, which read, "I am no longer a virgin. I had sex for the first time last night." I shuddered at the thought.

So, it's really no wonder that I took my time getting dressed, trying to arrive as late as possible at the event. Zain entered the bedroom agitatedly. My mother-in-law had just called to find out where we were for the fifteenth time – I knew, because I had been counting. Razia was complaining that all the guests had arrived and lunch was about to be served.

"Nadia, please, we have to get going. We're late for our own *Walimah*," Zain said urgently.

"I'm done," I admitted reluctantly and sprayed a whiff of perfume on my wrist before grabbing my blue, beaded purse from the night stand. "Let's go."

It's a thirty minute drive to Hawa Bibi and Yaseen's house, where the *walimah* was held. We were about to take the off-ramp leading into Lenasia, when the traffic suddenly came to a standstill. Zain strained his neck out the window to see what the problem was.

"Shit, there's a bloody road block," he cursed angrily and banged his fists on the steering wheel. Just then his cell phone rang and he answered, irritated. "We're almost there Mummy. There's a road block here just entering Lenz … yeah, I know. Just tell them to wait." He pressed the disconnect button hard and shoved the phone back into his pocket. I stared straight ahead, not wanting to aggravate him any further. The traffic moved slowly on and we drove past the metro police cautiously. The road cleared and Zain sped the rest of the way, screeching to a halt outside a double-story beige house with ostentatious gold-plated pillars and white palisades at the entrance. There were cars parked along the length of the street and around the block, too.

When we entered, family members, most of whom I did not recognise, crowded around me.

"Are you ok? You must be so tired. Can we get you anything?" they asked consolingly.

I nodded and smiled politely and took a seat at the table assigned to Zain and me. I noticed that everyone was a little more relaxed and cheerful than they had been at the wedding and I soon fell into a state of quiet comfort, just watching everyone around me fuss and chatter loudly.

"Welcome to the family!" Hawa Bibi came out from the adjacent room to greet me. She was dressed in a gold, beaded panjabi and sandals with straps. Her curly, black hair was arranged around her head and she wore a pair of large, hooped earrings that jingled when she spoke.

"Thank you," I replied. "You've done a great job," I added, gesturing towards the decor.

"You think so?" she asked rhetorically, pulling a chair to sit next to me. "We did our best, you know, Shaaista and I. That reminds me, you should try some of the desserts and pastries. Shaaista's a wonder in the kitchen. Everyone knows that. She used to take orders until a while ago, before university became too demanding."

I spotted Shaaista carrying a plate of mini Swiss rolls to the buffet table. She was dressed in a stylish blue dress and ballet pumps. I looked down at my own blue dress in dismay and thought that she looked more like the bride than what I did.

"I'll definitely have to taste some of her delights," I told Hawa Bibi, who was watching my expression closely.

"Do you bake?" she asked, as if it had suddenly dawned on her. "Zain loves his cream cakes and baklava."

I shook my head. "I'm not much of a baker or a cook, to tell you the truth, although I do sometimes get in the mood to make something delicious. That's mostly when I'm craving for it and there's no way of getting to a bakery or ordering take out."

Hawa Bibi looked at me aghast but didn't say anything – she had obviously expected something different from me. She stood up abruptly and put a hand on my shoulder.

"If you need anything don't hesitate to ask," she said. "I'm just going to check up on the cook to make sure everything's running smoothly."

I watched her approach Shaaista as she made her way to the kitchen, and whisper something into her ear. Shaaista glanced at me and waved.

I realised, as I sat there alone, that Zain had disappeared and that I had not yet greeted my mother-in-law. So as not to be rude, I got up and went in search of them. In the kitchen I found two helpers bent over the sink, scrubbing dishes, and the cook hurriedly rushing about, dishing out refills of biryani. A few male family members and Hawa Bibi were waiting to serve the biryani to the guests. I went to the back of the building to look for Zain but he was not there, either. I spotted Yaseen with a tray of empty water glasses. Without even greeting, Yaseen savagely pushed the tray into my hands.

"Nadia, please take these in. Tell Hawa Bibi that the service out here is shocking and that we need more womenfolk to clear up and do refills."

I nodded dumbly and, just before he turned around to get back to his friends, asked, "Have you seen Zain or Mummy anywhere? I can't seem to find either of them."

Yaseen shrugged, "Have you tried the bedrooms?" He walked off and I went quickly to the kitchen with the tray. I instructed the helpers to clear the dishes from the tables and then made my way towards the bedrooms.

I felt strange walking through somebody else's house, but I had no choice. As I approached the master bedroom at the end of the passage, I heard voices. Closer to the door, I stopped and listened. My mother-in-law was speaking in a choked-up voice, as if she had been crying.

"I'm going to miss you so much, my son. Now there's going to be no place in your life for me, anymore," she whimpered. I could hear Zain's voice soothing her in a low whisper.

"You'll always be my number one lady," he said. "You are always first in my heart. Nadia will just have to accept that." There was a pause and I could picture the scene – Zain with his head on his mother's lap as she stroked his hair.

"Thank you my son. You're the best. That's why I love you so much."

I couldn't believe that Razia chose my *walimah* day to be so emotional. I considered Zain's words – I would need to accept Razia as his "number one lady" – what was that all about? I shook my head in disappointment and walked back to the table without him. I didn't want to hear any more.

My first week into marriage, I developed "honeymoon cystitis". I had told Zain that we needed to take everything slowly but he hadn't listened. Before leaving for honeymoon, the doctor ordered that we refrain from having sex for at least a week. Zain was annoyed, but he didn't say anything. Instead, he obsessed over the details of the journey.

"Have you made sure the GPS is connected?" he asked me, whilst he carefully loaded one of the suitcases into the boot of his Volvo.

"Yes," I replied for the third time.

"And did you remember to pack my swim-trunks and toothbrush?"

"Yes," I said again.

He went through the list of food and beverages that he had asked me to bring along and I nodded robotically in reply to all his questions. He had rented a week's accommodation at a self-catering apartment in Umhlanga. It had been over ten years since I had had the privilege of seeing the ocean and I was really looking forward to it. I couldn't wait to feel the sand between my toes and the cool, foamy seawater around my ankles. I shivered with delight as we got into the car and buckled up. I was so deeply involved in my fantasies of the beach that I didn't notice Zain's hand on my shoulder until he started shaking me wildly to get my attention.

"Nadia, what's wrong with you? I've asked you twice already to punch the co-ordinates into the GPS!" he snapped.

"I'm s … sorry," I stuttered, his sharp tone tearing through my thoughts.

I punched in the co-ordinates to The Cabanas and then sat back to enjoy the trip. We didn't speak much for the first bit of the journey and I yawned sleepily.

"I hope you're not planning to sleep," he said sharply, looking at me out the corners of his eyes. "I need you to be alert and make sure that I don't lose concentration."

"Don't worry, I'll stay awake," I reassured him.

But we had woken up at three in the morning to get an early start and I was so sleepy that I barely managed to keep my eyes open. The radio was dead and when I tried striking up a conversation, Zain put his finger to his lips to silence me.

"No talking. I need to concentrate, Nadia. Do you have any idea how many accidents take place on this very same road every year? It's unbelievable," he explained.

Not having many choices to keep me awake, I scrounged at the bottom of my handbag for the chocolate I had bought earlier at Spar. I munched on it, knowing from my days at university that eating keeps you awake for at least an hour. I considered offering Zain a bite, but felt a little too greedy to share. Fortunately, he had nothing to say about my bit of selfish bingeing although, with every bite I took, I could imagine his reprimand – "Don't you know that chocolate will go straight to your hips? You'll end up looking like a cow." I shuddered. Zain was even in my subconscious. There was no escaping. I crumpled the empty wrapper in my fist and pushed it into the pocket of my jeans.

There was a deafening silence between us and I kept myself occupied with the scenery, taking note of the farmhouses and grazing cattle as we drove further from the city centre, into the countryside. It was a tiring drive, with little companionship, but I managed to keep my wits intact until we reached Montrose, the famous halfway "eat-and-take-a-leak" stop between Johannesburg and Durban. Zain parked the car a few feet from the main entrance and told me to meet him at the halaal take away, a small Muslim-run joint, well known for its chips-and-polony specials. I watched as he reversed the car to refuel the tank and check the tyre pressure. My legs felt like jelly as I walked along the paved pathway to the toilets. The queue was long and when I got to the shop Zain was already there, sitting at a table with two toasted sandwiches and cold drinks. I was ready to hear him complain about my taking too long in the bathrooms, but to my surprise he smiled the same winning smile that had captured my heart on our first date.

"Take a seat," he said, gesturing to the chair across him. "I took the liberty of ordering for you. I hope you don't mind?"

I returned the smile and sat down. "I'm not fussy," I replied as I took a large bite out of my sandwich. The flavour danced in my mouth and I found myself gobbling down the meal more quickly than I expected. Zain watched me with interest.

"I love a woman with an appetite," he said, with his mouth half-full.

"I know," I replied. "You said that the first time we had a meal together, remember?"

"How could I forget that day?" he said, sweetly, and reached out to touch my hand.

I felt a rush of affection course through my body, thinking that perhaps he was not good company only when driving long distances. We stared lovingly at each another, until his cell phone rang and the moment ended.

"Yes Mummy, we're safe. We've just stopped to stretch our legs and get something to eat," he said into the mouthpiece. He then looked at me briefly and turned to his right so that I couldn't see his face when he spoke again. "No, she didn't make padkos. Yes, I'll tell her that it's better if she does on our way back. Ok then. Speak to you later." He switched the phone off and I immediately noticed the change in his mood.

"How is Mummy?" I asked.

"She's ok. Just feeling a little flu-ish," he replied distantly. "We've got to get a move on, otherwise we'll miss half a day's worth of vacation."

I grabbed my handbag and followed him down the steps to where the car was parked. I looked at my wristwatch and was thankful for the half an hour of normality. I reassured myself that the next two hours would fly by.

The hours did not fly by. Zain was in a terrible mood and his anger was directed at me, the reason for which I could not be sure. The newspaper that I had bought at the Quick Shop was limply curled into a roll at my feet. I couldn't make it past the front page.

By the time we reached Durban's outskirts, I could smell and taste the sticky, salty sea air. I opened the window and felt the heat rush in. Zain's mood improved – I could sense the tension lifting. We drove past the palm trees growing on the islands on the highway and took the off-ramp to Umhlanga. As we made our way down the steep slope to The Cabanas, following the directions of the GPS voice command, I caught a glimpse of the aquamarine water below – it sparkled in the sunlight, like a million dancing stars.

There were families – men, women and children – wearing bikinis and shorts, walking along the pavement towards the entrance to the beach and it seemed as though, like us, everybody was on vacation, even though it was the off-peak season and schools were in the middle of their third term exams.

We reached our destination, a cream and white building soaring towards the sky, surrounded by palm trees on the ground level and a large, blue, glitzy sign that read "The Cabanas". Zain offloaded the luggage whilst I went inside to the reception desk to sign us in and collect the apartment's keys. They were short-staffed and the elevators were also being serviced, inconveniently, so we were forced to carry all our belongings up the stairs to the second floor. By the time we got to the door of the apartment I was hot, sweaty and looking forward to getting to the beach.

Apartment 20A was spacious and neat. There was a white and blue kitchen, in theme with the ocean, and printed palm trees on the walls to set the mood. There was a small lounge with a balcony overlooking the beach and a master bedroom with an en-suite bathroom. Zain dumped the cooler bag with all the groceries and frozen meat on the kitchen counter and stretched his arms above his head.

"This place is awesome," he said. He walked past me to the balcony. "I think I'll go for a quick swim."

He then went into the bedroom to change. Excitedly, I followed him. I was in the process of unzipping the side pocket of my suitcase to retrieve my swimming costume when he came out of the bathroom in his shorts. He stopped abruptly and looked at me in confusion.

"What are you doing, Nadia?" he asked curtly.

"I'm joining you," I replied, smiling from ear to ear. "I can't wait to dip my feet into the water."

He tipped his head to one side in disapproval.

"Are you planning to wear that?" he eyed the black and red full-bodied swimming costume I held in my hand.

I nodded.

"No. I won't have my wife parading like some cheap 'Western' woman in front of a whole lot of men, wearing nothing but a skin-tight, sleeveless, leg-revealing item of clothing that leaves nothing to the imagination." He shook his head. "If you want to join me on the beach I suggest that you get hold of one of those Islamic costumes that cover you from head to toe or better yet, just hold up your jeans and take a dip."

I glared at him angrily. If I'd known he was so particular about my dress code, I would have brought something else to wear with me. I had an outfit at home that would have been suitable for swimming and which I was sure he would have approved of. It had been given to me by my Aunty in the hope that Allah would grant me *hidayat* to start donning the veil.

I put the black and red swimming costume away reluctantly and closed the suitcase. I decided to go to the beach in what I was wearing instead – a pair of faded blue jeans and a T-shirt supporting the Society for Animals in Distress.

I was at his heels, following him out the front door, when he turned around abruptly, his face inches from mine, and asked, "When will lunch be ready?"

In shock, I realised that the time was already 12:45 and Zain liked to eat at 13:30.

"What would you like to eat?" I asked. I knew that I didn't have enough time to go to the beach, come back and have lunch ready on time. I decided to let the swimming pass for now.

"Steak and mashed potato," he replied without thinking twice.

I couldn't believe it. Zain already had a menu planned in his head! I watched him leave, and started preparing the meal. As I peeled the potatoes, I realised that I was still nervous about my cooking and Zain had not as yet given me any indication that my food was to his liking. "The way to a man's heart is through his stomach," is the common saying repeated throughout all Indian households.

Half an hour later, the food was cooking and Zain had still not returned. I took the opportunity to freshen up and change into a white cotton dress that I had hoped to wear ever since I had heard about our trip to the coast, two months before. When I was done, I went to the balcony to look at the holidaymakers below. There were a few people walking along the paved pathway which ran parallel to the ocean line, whilst others were buying Dinky Doughnuts from the red-capped man who stood behind a stand. There were swimmers gathered along the water's edge, and holidaymakers relaxed under multi-coloured umbrellas, half exposed to the sun for a mild tan.

I stared into the distance, my mind drifting in the direction of a sailing boat and, as I was imagining myself as one of the lucky passengers on board, I felt Zain's muscular arms encircle my waist from behind. I jumped, a little startled, and slowly turned around to face him. His skin was already a shade darker and there was a calm, blissful smile on his face.

"Did you miss me?" he whispered in my ear. I shivered at the sensual tone of his voice.

"Yes," I replied.

"I have something for you." He reached into his back pocket and pulled out a turquoise and black beaded bracelet. "There was a woman selling it downstairs and I thought it would look lovely on your wrist".

I studied the bracelet in astonishment. "It's beautiful," I admitted in a low voice, tracing the beads with my finger. "Thank you."

He smiled and kissed me, "You're welcome. I love you, Nadia."

I felt my heart beat gently and replied, "I love you too, Zain".

I didn't go to the ocean at all during that trip. It so happened that after we had eaten lunch, the weather changed – it became stormy and cold and it drizzled the entire week. I was disappointed, but figured it wasn't all that bad because Zain was good to me. He was more attentive to my needs and even went as far as switching off his cell phone, so that we could spend quality time with one another without being disturbed. He also spoilt me by taking me out to two fancy restaurants so that I didn't have to cook. It was awesome being pampered in that way. The drive back to Johannesburg wasn't that bad either, although Zain did request that I pack some sandwiches for us to eat on the way; a bit of friendly advice from his mother, he mentioned. We only stopped once on the way back home, at a filling station near Harrismith, to stretch our legs. We ate our lunch in the car and drove back to Fordsburg in four hours.

It felt strange to return home after the holiday. It was all too overwhelming. I reminded myself that it would take time to get used to being a married woman and dealing with all the responsibilities that come with being a "model" Muslim Indian wife. Zain and I would soon be following some kind of routine: going to work in the morning and coming home to prepare dinner, Zain exhausted and wanting his meal on time … then sitting in front of the television and falling asleep.

I smiled. I could just picture it. The mundane and ordinary life we would be leading in the weeks ahead. It was comforting in a way, because that's how a home is built, upon the ordinary … I sighed. I unpacked the suitcases and sorted out the leftover groceries, whilst Zain slept on the couch. I watched as his chest heaved rhythmically. I felt like cuddling up next to him, but there was still too much that I needed to do. I got a blanket from the linen cupboard to throw over him. I could not keep my eyes off his peaceful face … Eventually, however, I managed to force myself away and switch off the light. Tomorrow would be another day …

"Pull yourself together!" – battling depression in pregnancy

Mymoena Arnold

Solitude accompanies me at every turn.
I welcome the silence that descends within, drowning out the voices that refuse to let me be.
Darkness comes. It blankets and shrouds every crevice of light. I retreat deeper into the abyss of nothing.
I yearn to reach the point of no return. But the journey there is arduous and taxing.
To nowhere. To nothing. To where the damned roam free and the past is held at bay.
I need so badly to belong somewhere.
I hear voices in the distance. I hold the palms of my hands to both ears, willing them to stop. I start rocking on my knees, back and forth. The voices will not stop. Why will they not stop? For goodness sake, make them stop. They become louder. Closer.
A scream pierces the still, silent, darkened room.
A door flies open.
Bodies rush in.
Light. Someone has switched on my light.
I turn my face to the wall.
Dark, but oh, so familiar. Inviting. So safe. Home.

At the age of twenty-seven, I was expecting my second child. A routine visit to the family physician revealed this exciting news. Happiness and laughter flowed all round. My joy was short lived, however, when I started spotting the next week. My husband took me to my gynecologist, who suggested doing an ultrasound.

The visit to the radiologist was filled with trepidation and apprehension on my part. I could feel the knots in my tummy. I felt physically ill. During the ultrasound, the radiologist told me that it seemed as if I had miscarried, pointing to dark spots on the monitor.

I felt like a freight train had rammed into me. My hands and legs went completely numb, and my palms were sweating in an eighteen-degree, air-conditioned room. The silence was so deafening, it felt as though my heartbeat was roaring like tidal waves in my ears. Then every joint started to tingle and suddenly my nerves felt frayed and taut. The moment I walked out of that room, I collapsed against my husband in total despair. I cried and cried and cried. I cried when we met with the gynecologist. I cried on my way home that day. I cried throughout that night. I cried for the next ten days to follow. By the time we saw the gynecologist again and he confirmed life within me, it was way too late. Those careless words in the radiology room had unwittingly spurred my entry into the world of depression. The months that followed were beyond my control.

In the first month I started losing the desire to eat, bath or work. My hubby kept telling me to "pull myself together". I tried. I really did, but I could not rekindle my zest for life. It had somehow gone "A.W.O.L." on me. After a while I started resenting those words – to "pull myself together" – and would freak out every time I heard them. One day, in a flat panic, I called my father out of his medical practice to ask him to have a father-son chat with hubby. That night my father counselled my hubby about depression and its debilitating effects on the sufferer, advising that the best response was unconditional support.

The rest of our family stayed well clear of me in the months to follow. It seems they had no clue on how to deal with my sudden lapse and were traumatised by my rapid decline, both mentally and physically. I lost weight, lots of it. I neglected to take care of my outward appearance, and had no problem walking around in pajamas the whole day – the whole week – without bathing, too. I failed to comb my hair, cut my nails, or brush my teeth. As my mental state worsened, these basic daily sanitary and hygienic practices were done for me by my husband or domestic helper.

In the second month I started waking up in the middle of the night and pacing the passages of my home with my arms raised on either side. I could no longer sit still for long periods or lie down with ease; I would always be fidgety and restless – pacing, always pacing. Every joint, from head to toe, twitched with pins and needles. Feelings of anxiety crippled any steady movements I once had, and I slowed down into an awkward shuffling of feet and half-bent body. It was at this point that my husband realised there was something seriously wrong with my mental health. I think the sight of me pacing the passages in that manner was a scene straight out of a mental asylum. With a strong recommendation from the gynecologist, we made an appointment with a psychiatrist. I had to undergo many psychiatric consultations and psychological evaluation and tests. I was put on high-dose anti-depressants that sedated me, so that initially I lapsed into an almost zombie-like state.

During the following months I remember my daughter stroking my hair and rubbing my hands. She would talk in a soothing, soft tone all the time. I felt her doing that. I saw her doing that. I heard her doing that, but I never uttered a word. I had no feeling for her. It did not matter to me whether she was there or not. I did not care in the slightest.

I was regularly admitted to hospital to be fed intravenously, since I barely ate, leaving me in a constantly dehydrated state. With no sustenance for myself, there was no nourishment for the baby to thrive on. Hospital care was frequent and nightmarish. Today, just the thought of sitting on a hospital bed unnerves me.

During my sixth month of pregnancy I turned suicidal. I started throwing myself on the ward floor, tummy first. I just wanted it out. The baby. I just needed it out of me. I did not want to be pregnant any longer; I do not know why. I just felt that and acted on it. Cascading emotions overwhelmed me and seemed to lock themselves in my very being, determined to wreak havoc with my psyche. All I had left to latch on to were feelings of worthlessness, despair, disinterest, disillusionment and distress, resulting in regular panic attacks, anxiety episodes, and dark thoughts that speedily welled up. I was stuck in a big, black hole, trying to crawl my way out, saddled with all these terrifying feelings. The less those around me understood, the further I fell into this hole.

One night, the team of doctors assigned to my care called my father and husband to inform them that my mental and physical condition was worsening, and, at this rate, there was little else they could do other than increase the dosage of the anti-depressants and perhaps administer some electro-shock therapy. My father was determined I would not have any electrodes stuck to my head, sending electric jolts that could spell further mental anguish and brain scarring later on in life for me. I remember him ushering everyone out of the hospital room and coming to sit beside me on the bed. He looked down at me, tears started to run down his cheeks and he said in a quiet, trembling voice, "My baby, Muslims do not commit suicide." I do not know if it was his tears or what he said, or a combination of both, but it left a profound imprint on my brain, and I stopped throwing myself on the floor. Whatever explanation there is for such a dramatic turnaround, and I am sure there is one, I personally cannot define it. Verily, the Almighty knows best.

On one of my routine gynecological check-ups I complained to the doctor about feeling movement similar to that of contractions. He duly examined me, ran a few tests and decided to admit me overnight for observation. During the night the contractions became stronger and fewer apart. I remember the look of shock on his face the next morning when he read the overnight report. It seemed I had gone into full labour and there was not a thing anyone could do to delay or prevent it. Of course, this news also left the rest of my family in total shock.

Well, like it or not, at six and a half months since his conception, my son would be making his way into this world.

The birth was quick and so easy, probably because the epidural did a magnificent job, as always, and I thought here is my chance to finally get this baby out of me. Pushing him out of me felt like a huge burden had been lifted off my shoulders. I enjoyed a feeling of exhilaration and relief – not because I had a healthy, newborn son, but because he was finally out and I could get back to dealing with just me.

The arrival of my son, after he had spent the first two weeks of his infant life in neonatal ICU, was cause for much celebration in our household. I had no interest in the new arrival and saw him as a hindrance to my needs and wants. Could no-one understand that I wanted to be alone? This little person was invading my space. I needed to be alone with my darkness, surrounded by long periods of silence.

My husband, who had juggled my illness by playing the roles both of mummy and daddy to our daughter before our son was born, now had to assume all the other maternal responsibilities that came with a newborn. It was a traumatic and exhausting period for him, as well. He did not have the luxury of breaking down at any point. He had no choice but to keep strong for the children and me. With the help of my father, he kept it all together. I must also pay homage to my sister-in-law, Zainab. She was a pillar of strength and cushion of comfort during my lowest period, *Ramadaan* 2001.

Till this day, when I look upon my son, waves of guilt overwhelm me and I feel so ashamed. I worry about the day he will ask about his birth – what then? What will go through his mind when he hears about the events leading up to his birth? I was experiencing a major depressive episode. The magnitude of human suffering this illness brings is incomprehensible.

Our daughter suffered the most. She endured deep psychological scars that led to her also experiencing nervous episodes and bouts of childhood anxiety. She has been for counselling since then, and has improved tremendously. Still, she had to grow up too quickly in that dark period. Too quickly for a four-year-old. This is a silent torment that will plague me for the rest of my life.

It took two-and-half-years are what it took for me to return to what was a shadow of my former self. Eight years thereafter, I was divorced. My marriage had deteriorated due to the pressures and stresses of this illness. At first, feeling like a complete failure, I blamed myself. I was no longer a size thirty-two, ambitious, bright-eyed, sexually-able young wife. The consequence of my recurrent depressive disorder had left me with a few extra kilos, scared of taking risks, withdrawn, emotionally reclusive and sexually stunted.

After some time I learned to accept the loss of my marriage. You can love someone a lot, but they might not end up being the partner you need in life. And – as one is meant to do with every setback in life – I chose to learn from my mistakes, and to use the lesson towards improving my psyche and outward appearance. Experiences like mine are life-altering by their very nature. Embrace the experiences and you will be the richer for it. Resist and all will surely be lost.

I find that I can no longer tolerate conflict-laden situations or everyday pressures with the same gumption and resolve I had before my depression. I doubt that anyone who endures such serious depression in pregnancy ever fully recovers. But, as a loyal servant of the Almighty, I believe that keeping the faith goes a long way to staying sane and strong.

I also believe that society has to revisit and retract the stigma it has placed on victims of mental health illnesses. This form of illness is on the same scale as other illnesses, such as cancer or liver disease, where the condition becomes chronic and at times completely debilitating. There are various methods of treatment and therapy to resolve mental health issues. Most importantly though, victims should never be made to feel guilty if they are unable to perform the tasks and honour the duties they could prior to the onset of their mental illness. I spent a lot of unnecessary time second-guessing and blaming myself for everything that went wrong when I was diagnosed with recurrent depressive disorder. Only after many years and many upsetting incidents could I patch together a quilt of life experiences that wove a powerful message of survival, hope and fervent faith.

The restoration of my mental health, bearing in mind I could experience lapses, was dependent on familial support, empathy and patience. Knowledge, coupled with understanding, can strengthen bonds. Unfortunately, this was not entirely forthcoming, and led to many situations where misinterpretation and miscommunication were rife. Prescription drugs were merely there to stabilise my medical condition and could not alter the ignorance of many, force anyone to provide empathy and support, nor ensure that anyone would remain patient and reassuring. Medication also could not quell bouts of frustration and lessen periods of dissatisfaction.

The best thing you can do to help anyone who suffers from a mental health illness is to remain understanding, supportive, kind and respectful of the sufferer's limitations. Every person deserves the right to be happy and feel fulfilled in their lives. No-one causes or asks for a mental health illness. Many factors contribute to its onslaught, and religion, culture and ignorance are the main antagonists in the fight against its stigma. As a Muslim wife and daughter-in-law I was expected to "pull myself together" on numerous occasions. My road to recovery was long, taxing and lonely. So many arguments could have been avoided – so many misconceptions too – had people only taken the time to understand the effects of my mental health illness. But, often, judgement was swift and final. I stood no chance against eons of indoctrination and skewed perceptions. Familial support was conditional and withdrawn at will. For a long time the bottled-up hurt, deep-seated anger and irrational resentment spilled over. Thankfully this too has been resolved with some narrative and cognitive therapy sessions, enabling the simple act of forgiveness and mercy, along with the ardent desire to live a contented and peaceful life.

So much time has lapsed since that awful, fateful day in the radiology room. I am currently the mother to two beautiful kids of my own, and to four boys from my husband's previous union. Yes, I remarried three-and-a-half years after my divorce. I found someone who was willing to ride the waves with me forever, and who did not mind getting soaking wet, under the most adverse conditions. Hallid tends to every emotional need I have. He constantly reassures me, waits on me like a queen and protects me fiercely. Since I have had him in my life, I have not experienced another depressive episode.

Every day I wake up motivating myself with an encouraging word and religious thought. Some days are a walk in the park; some days are difficult and too long; some days are in between; some days are blissful. No day is ever the same.

Despite my ordeal, I feel blessed to be able to live a meaningful life with my "six-pack": Ayesha, Umr, Naim, Mogamad Zain, Mogamad Idris and Hasan. I must make special mention of Ayesha and Mogamad Zain, who were the innocent casualties of my illness during rough days and rougher nights, when I was often withdrawn and at times unaffectionate. The mood swings and snappish retorts only drew them closer to me, made them more loyal and developed a kind of fortitude within them that amazes me to this day. Bless their beautiful souls. I am thankful for the past, for those who shared it with me but could not walk the distance. I look forward to a bright future built on every memory that shaped the woman I am today. I live in the present, forever mindful that life is short and unpredictable. So, leave nothing to chance. Make your dreams happen. Make your efforts count. Make people understand. Make changes that matter and that complete you. Make a great life for yourself. Be who you really are.

Finally, a heartfelt thank you to my father, who inspired me to will myself to live, and who stuck by me, venturing through the corridors of my darkest moments right alongside me. I never realised that the light I sought was standing right next to me all the time. Love you, Daddy.

"Pull yourself together." Oh how I wish it could have been that simple!

Motherly instinct

Naseema Moolla

I feel him in my head; he is almost like liquid fire that courses through my veins. That familiar voice that, when I hear it, makes me smile from deep inside. I inhale the scent of his shirt, the one he wore to work – a breezy mixture of sweet spices – that familiar odour. I can distinguish the sounds that remind me of him: a footfall in the hay, a stamp on my newly furbished tiles, a yawn in the night, a whisper in my ear, the purr of his car as he swerves into the driveway. I feel him in my head and in my heart. It's like my every heartbeat thrums his name and every vein that courses through my body throbs like midnight heat. When he looks at me after the day is done and the night is fresh, I smile; I am content. When he presses his body against me, I swirl. I swirl, I unfurl and every look is a mystery, every scent a heady blend of years of passion, love, tears, joys, pain, victories, tragedies and treasures.

I glance at him. And I am so thankful to Allah for him: my husband, my precious love. When he shaves his hair he looks all minty and refreshed – boyish and very smart. I adore his smile when his lips curve into a mischievous but saucy arc that can rock my inner core into a molten volcanic eruption that sends shocks and shudders right through to places I never knew existed. I ponder back to those precious moments when he lightly tapped my shoulder, when he accidentally brushed his hand across my cheek, when he lifted my veil and ran his fingers across my lips. I'm lost in those memories … Yet, in all these moments of emotion I still feel every pain that has stung me and am thankful that he stood by me.

My husband was my pillar of strength through every waking moment of trying to be motherly. After Ahmed was born, I succumbed to post-natal depression – severe emotional, psychological and physical trauma that sent me reeling from baby crib to confinement room. The caesarian section wound singed and sizzled each time I moved or yawned or cried or fed. My son was perfect in every way – and still is – but my mind and emotions blinded me. My motherly instinct did not kick in. Breastfeeding did not happen, I was highly constipated, I was highly emotional and I burst into tears each time anybody mentioned "Mickey Mouse".

Adding to my depression was the fact that my husband had a date with the worst of sluts, unemployment. She danced with him and wrapped her talons around his biceps, she swirled like a dancer around him and taunted him with her raving red hair, she embraced him and I was horrified. I drowned in an abyss of anxiety about not managing to care for my baby. I was bludgeoned by worries of running out of baby lotion, milk formula or disposable napkins. It was madness. I had forgotten that the hand of the Almighty was larger.

I waited for the moment when I would burst with that peachy, motherly glow that every other woman who had given birth seemed to have. I waited for my arms to enjoy cradling my infant son. I looked for a reason to smile at him and I … couldn't. Clocks ticked, time travelled, baby feeds were carried out with precision, growers buttoned up, navel tied, circumcision fussed over, *aqeeqa* passed, mutton dished out, in-laws "cooed" over Ahmed. Still I waited for that burst of sunlight which a mother feels for her child. But I remained the stand-offish mother, sautéing in some sort of unpleasant, obtuse world.

People were undergoing worse kinds of catastrophes. It was April 2003, the beginning stages of George Bush's manoeuvering and manipulation into Iraq. My son was born at the precise time when the USA declared war upon the people of the sand dunes. I vividly recall disturbing images of Casspirs on desert sand; bulky GI men hiding behind masks; helpless civilians in torn cotton *kurtas*, staring doom in the face; and mothers whose tears streamed down their dusty faces awaiting their destiny.

My serpentine mind danced with me. What about the mothers left behind in the dusk and dark when rapid fire burst around them and strange men invaded their homes? How could babies be born at a time when war signified intense hatred and hurt between people? I always imagined babies brought with them flower petals, fragrant and soft. I could not imagine a dusty infant sprayed with blood. I could not picture a mother bringing the miracle of life to a battle zone, surrounded by enemies who understood nothing of her culture. I wept as I thought about the fathers who were not there to receive their newborns because they were recruited in the war, slashing at a giant.

April 2003 brought with it a gloom that unfolded like a moth's wing over my heart and mind. I may have been a mother who was safe and secluded, loved and warm, cloistered, and showered with gifts and attention, but there was this crazy something that incessantly gnawed at me. Each time I felt a stir of delight, the dark winged moth spread its venomous cloth over me. There was a hollow deep within me, a restless ache that no one but my *Creator* could soothe.

The emptiness stayed with me for a long time. Perhaps it was the responsibility of having to take care of this new person with whom I had been blessed. Ultimately, having a baby is a huge responsibility. The moment you set eyes upon the little creature, everything changes. Every world view, every philosophy, everything you see, hear, taste and breathe alters. My days – as do those of so many other new mothers – became a blend of perceptions consumed by guilt, a sense of abandonment, listlessness and emptiness. I faced a mountain. I had to climb. There were jagged edges that cropped out everywhere. Where was my motherly instinct?

Our older Indian generation considers post-natal depression a taboo. Mothers don't behave in "that way", especially Muslim mothers. "*Arre*, what, *beti*?" exclaimed *Nanima*. "There is no such word. These doctors don't know anything. *Beti,* we have all had children. You can't behave like this. It is improper." "Improper", just like divorce is improper and buying takeout is improper and asking the father of the child to change a diaper or get up for a feed is improper. Taboos and "impropers" – things that came on the *Truro*[v] with indentured labourers – were they ordinary or were they all just my fault? After all, I was the designated drama queen in the family.

Mummy said one day, "It's normal, it happens. You should speak to a professional and get some help, some therapy." Alas, I could not, I just could not and I did not. I was too embarrassed to get treatment. What would *Nanima* think? Hence, as the days melted into seasons and the seasons simmered into years, while leaves turned rusty and global warming changed weather patterns, my son grew up. Ahmed became, *Alhamdullilah*, a strapping nine year old who is my purest delight. And my husband remained my handsome, raging warrior, my strength.

Until that day …

I awoke that day and realised that I was lost; we were both lost. We had vanished into some concrete city smog that had swallowed us whole and clogged our ventricles, the parts of the heart that carry our blood, love, life and romance. Romance, love, life and heart were a bit distant – after all, the ventricles were clogged, not vanquished, just clogged and too complex to re-open.

It should have come as no surprise that, having been knotted together for fourteen years, battling with the extremities of emotions, trapped in daily routines, challenged with the pressures of the outside world and work, our relationship had become laced with the unfiltered and fully weighted demands of life. It is because of this timeline of life, routine and shapeless days that we forgot about loving.

I have observed that at some point in many relationships, couples communicate in deathly syllables that would make an iceberg melt; syllables that create their own language, marked by long, eerie silences that can beat time to a pulp. Recalling our amazing matrimonial past, I never thought that I would succumb to endless silences that shatter like a million splintering pieces of silver glitter to stab me deep down in my soul. I thought those syllables would never describe me, would never describe our marriage, because between us we have Ahmed. And because of him, we will laugh, love and feel – individually, with him, for now – but, soon, together, again.

Ahmed is my life, my core and I will strive for the best for him. And I guess, in making this decision for my son, my motherly instinct has finally engulfed me. And for that I am forever thankful.

Divorce was not an option

Anonymous

My story begins at the innocent age of seventeen, when I entered the world of university. There I was, just out of school, embracing the big, bad world. Coming from a Muslim school, I found myself not well educated about other religions and the world out there. I chose to study biokinetics, a course that not many Muslims take. I was therefore forced to make friends with male students as well as students from other races. I found the task of socialising with others a fascinating venture but at the same time I felt oddly deprived, as I had previously socialised with only female Muslim Indians. Nonetheless, I made the best of friends and fitted right in – and that was my first challenge as a young Muslim woman!

My naivety was met with much criticism. I was shocked and horrified at the stories my friends would tell me. Yes, some Muslims do consume alcohol and, yes, some Muslims do engage in pre-marital sex and, yes, some of the Mr Eligibles that I would meet would have attempted taking drugs. I had no idea about all of this, as I had been kept sheltered behind the walls of my school. I armed myself with some basic knowledge of how people function and behave. I warned myself that everyone around me was not as innocent and pure as I perceived and I was determined to maintain my beliefs, no matter what.

I wore a headscarf in my first year of university study but this change in dress code only lasted six months, as I was not completely ready for it. I met my husband in my second year of study and it was love at first sight. With pressure from my family and in line with "doing the right thing", we got married after graduation. I was doing my internship at the time and my husband was doing his articles. What we earned as a combined salary in our first year of marriagc is what we presently pay for rent on our house!

Marriage came with many challenges. We both had to adjust to each others' families, habits and mood swings. We fought almost every day about almost everything. I tried in my marriage but I knew that something was amiss – this was not the man with whom I had fallen in love! The man I had fallen in love with did not get angry over insignificant things; he did not throw objects around when things did not go his way; and he certainly was not so pushy.

When I sought solace, I was met with the most bizarre responses. I was told that if my husband apologised, everything would return to normal. I kept my problems away from my parents as I did not want to worry them. I come from a strict family background and, for me, divorce was not an option. My husband, on the other hand, did consider divorce or separation as options. I was worried that people would speak negatively about me. What would everyone think if my marriage failed? Once again, I blamed my naive upbringing, which taught me to believe that divorce was not the solution. I am now so thankful that I was brought up with these beliefs because, had I not persevered, we would not have gotten to the point where my husband was diagnosed with bipolar mood disorder. There was finally an explanation for all the fighting, pain, and tears!

Our lives changed after the diagnosis. We were happy for the first time in a very long time. I no longer hid behind a fake smile. We got both of our families involved as well as many medical personnel. I am certain that without the support I received from my family, my marriage would not have survived, and I would be writing this as a divorced woman.

As if juggling marriage, our new careers, family dynamics and our new-found financial obligations wasn't enough, four months after getting married, I fell pregnant. A blessing in disguise; an unplanned miracle! I am grateful for the son with whom I have been blessed. I am constantly reminded that I love this boy so much that it actually pains me! I often say there is not enough space in my heart for the love I have for my Hamza.

It was so easy the first time round and I was sure that baby number two would work out perfectly. I was so wrong. Over the past four years we have lost four babies through miscarriages and one ectopic pregnancy. We are trying everything we can to have more children and I know that soon our *duahs* will be granted and we will overcome infertility.

It was these major, life-changing events that got me to rethink my faith. How could I expect Allah to give me all I desired when I wasn't half the Muslim I should be? I wore my headscarf once again, and armed myself with prayer, faith and hope to face the world.

I now work in an environment where many of my patients are from other faiths. The same questions are asked time and time again. "Did your husband make you wear this? Why?" They go to the extent of inferring that I may be a different person to the one I was before. My answer is simple – I wear the headscarf for me and only for me. I have changed; my eyes are now opened. I am more aware of the fact that nothing is in our control and Allah will only give us what we can manage. In my heart, I remain the same carefree, loving, full-of-energy woman I have always been.

I am now at the peak of my life, my marriage and my career. I have achieved so much as a biokineticist. I have a successful business and am on my way to obtaining my Master's degree. But my work will never take preference over my family. *Shukr Alhamdullilah*, I now have a successful marriage and I am a mother to a gorgeous little boy.

CONTRIBUTORS

Fatima Adam is a qualified educational psychologist. She enjoys reading good books and cooking exotic meals. She lives in Sandton with her husband and two children.

Mymoena Arnold is the owner of soft-skills training and life-skills workshops, The Business Zone. She is married to Hallid Smith and they have six beautiful children together. Her penchant for writing stems from her late mother, Ayesha Ahmed. She owes her desire to share and inspire to her father, Amien Arnold. Look out for her book entitled, *Pull Yourself Together, and Stepping Up the Game* – a practical guide on how to confront and cope with all things personally traumatic, while busting some myths along the way.

Zakiyyah Asmall is a single mum to an amazing little girl. She is studying towards a Bachelor of Commerce degree. She was raised in the small town of Newcastle and has a passion for art and mosaic.

Hasina Asvat grew up in Lenasia and presently resides there. She is a physiotherapist by profession. She enjoys art, travelling and spending time with her extended family.

Nadia Cassim is a qualified town and regional planner, and a practicing financial service representative. She is a firm believer of doing what makes you happy and following your dreams. Her passion for writing and art has encouraged her to complete a novel and host three Islamic art exhibitions over the past five years. She is also the editor of the progressive Muslim women's magazine, *Irtiqa.*

Quraisha Dawood published an anthology of poetry in 2002 called *Jewels of Faith.* Since then she has been a freelance journalist and political cartoonist. She has recently completed her master's degree on the relationships between Muslim madams and their maids in Durban. She is currently pursuing her PhD and she lectures at UKZN.

Somayya Hansrod is a mathematics teacher. Frying onions scares her but teaching long division does not. She lives in Roshnee with her husband Aadil and three children, Naailah, Uwais and Abdur Rahman.

Farhana Ismail is an optometrist and has an Honours degree in Journalism. She is a member of the Masjid-ul Islam working committee. She has been involved in numerous Masjid initiatives, including youth *halqahs*, the drafting of the Masjid's Muslim Marriages Bill submission to Parliament, and the *Ramadaan* feeding programme. She is also involved in a *madressa* which she runs from her home. This *madressa* has a vision to develop influential Muslim youth who are equipped to live Islam in a diverse and changing world, and able to make the Quranic message relevant to their time.

Saffiya Ismail is a blogger and a spiritualist. She is conservative and yet modern. She is a daydreamer, truth-seeker, sister-in-humanity, a writer and a proud Muslim woman. She had her own talk show on Radio Pietermaritzburg. Saffiya is a motivational speaker and writes articles for *Al Qalam* and the *Ladysmith Gazette*. She is also a contributor for Women 24.com and has also edited a book by Saleem Ahmed titled *Islam – A Religion of Peace*. Read more about Saffiya on her blog "Simply Me – Personified".

Zaheera Jina has a PhD in mathematics education. She grew up in Azaadville and now lives in Lenasia with her husband, two sons and many in-laws. She enjoys reading, writing and painting.

Adeela Kasoojee is first and foremost a mother, wife and daughter. She is an avid food blogger with a passion for cooking. She has much interest in children's rights, constitutional law and human rights law. Despite all these endeavours and working full time, she has much further to travel on her journey through life.

Jasmine Khan is a writer, motivational speaker and tutor of English. For four years she worked with a partner under the business name "Positive Energy Guide", facilitating workshops in the community on self-awareness, Islamic parenting and team building. In December 2010 she self-published her first book, *Experience the Flow*. She has been published on the Living Islam website and in the *Muslim Man* magazine in KwaZulu-Natal, and for three years she wrote the "Stop the cycle" column for *Muslim Views.* During 2011 she published a collection of these articles in book form, entitled *Behind Closed Doors*. The book poses the question, "How do we live in the light of the *Quran* and *Sunnah*?" She is currently in her second year of writing a new column for *Muslim Views*, entitled "From consciousness to contentment". She has two sons and five grandchildren and lives in Cape Town.

Sumaya Kola is a pulmonary hypertension warrior. She has a keen interest in Islamic literature, art and photography. She has a deep love for Palestine and hopes to serve as a humanitarian resource in Gaza some day.

Tazmin Mahomed grew up in Pretoria and now lives in Durban with her husband and four children. She loves reading, writing, philosophising, cooking and travelling. In dabbling with words she finds comfort, companionship and comprehension. She is the author of *Secrets of a Muslim Heart*, which is a collection of poetry and prose describing her journey into spiritual awakening.

Salma Mangera is a speech therapist by profession and wordsmith by choice. She lives in Lenasia with her husband Riaad and her daughter Attiya.

Sumayya Mehtar is a qualified emergency pharmacist currently residing in the Kingdom of Saudi Arabia within the Najd region. She grew up in a small town called Azaadville in South Africa. She comes from a family that is very compassionate towards the poor and the underprivileged and is active in charity work in various countries around the world, especially Malawi. All proceeds from her blog "Desert Moon's Diary" are given away to charity. She encourages one and all to take time out to view the blog and make a contribution towards the poor and needy.

Naseema Moolla is passionate about serving humanity through the written word. She strives to be the voice of those who do not have one. As an educator she also inspires and motivates the youth.

Zayboon Motala is a teacher by profession. She is involved in social work in South Africa and its neighbouring countries. She met with a bad accident and only walked again after eleven years of disability. She has a school named in her honour.

Rehana Moosajee was born in Ophirton and raised in Lenasia. She holds a teaching degree from the University of the Witwatersrand. She became actively involved in community structures and media and in 2000 became a local government councillor in the City of Johannesburg. Rehana is married to Salim and they have two children, Aadil and Faheema.

Nabeelah Patel is currently doing her Master's degree in International Relations at the University of the Witwatersrand. Her interests include literature, film, art and theatre. She aspires to promote world peace. Through her work as an activist, she aims to reach the level of a UN ambassador in the future.

Yasmin Denat holds a Bachelor of Arts with Honours in Publishing and Editing. The written word has always been her intense passion and her dreams of being a writer have never quite diminished. Yasmin lives in Azaadville and is the mother to three kindred souls.

Shireen Sabodien holds a degree in information technology. She is fiercely loyal and protective of her loved ones. She lives in Cape Town with her father and her two sons, Baizeed and Ijaaz.

Bibi-Aisha Wadvalla is an award winning journalist, who realised that pumps aren't the best footwear for covering revolutions. She's a bookworm, a teapot, and to her friends, a great cook. Her first love is Cairo, a city she calls her second home.

GLOSSARY

aaloobedda – (Gujerati) Indian dish made with potato and eggs
Aameen – (Arabic) declaration of affirmation of supplication
abaya – (Arabic) loose fitting cloak worn by Muslim women
ahre – (Gujerati) approximate
Ai poiri hu kare? – (Gujerati) What is this girl up to?
Al Bayhaqi – an author of a compilation of Hadith
Alhamdulillah – (Arabic) All praise be to Allah
Aalima – (Arabic) female Muslim scholar trained in Islam and Islamic law
AllahuAalam – (Arabic) Allah knows best
Al-Qalam – the name of a South African Muslim newspaper
Appa – (Arabic) name usually given to a female elder or teacher out of respect
aqeeqa – (Arabic) act of slaughtering either one or two sheep on the birth of a baby
Arafat – a mountain on the outskirts of Makkah where pilgrims gather to fulfill their rites during the Hajj
atchaar – (Hindi) Indian side dish of pickled vegetables mixed with masalas
ayat – (Arabic) verse in the holy Quran
Bajan –characteristic accent of Barbadians
bajee – (Gujerati) grandfather or elderly male person
barkhat – (Arabic) blessings
beti – (Gujerati) daughter
biryani – (Persian) rice dish made from spices, rice, mutton, chicken, fish or vegetables
bou oonchie – (Gujerati) too tall
burfee – (Persian) sweetmeat
burkah – (Arabic) loose, flowing garment intended to cover a woman's hair and body
champal – (Hindi) sandal
chana dhal – (Gujerati) dish made from lentils
chana flour – (Gujerati) flour made from ground chick peas
chotikhala – (Gujerati) mother's youngest sister
coloured – South African term for a person of mixed race

daada – (Gujerati) paternal grandfather
dadima – (Gujerati) paternal grandmother
da'wah – (Arabic) making an invitation to Islam
deen – (Arabic) religion
dhana-jeeroo – (Gujerati) spice mix of coriander and cumin
dhikr – (Arabic) reciting the praises of Allah and his beloved Prophet Muhammad (SAW)
doekie – (Afrikaans) headscarf
dorpie – (Afrikaans) small town
duah – (Arabic) act of supplication
Eid – Islamic celebration
Eid-Ul-Adha – Islamic celebration to commemorate the day on which Prophet Ibraheem (A.S) was ordered to sacrifice his son Isma'eel (A.S)
Eid-Ul-Fitr – Islamic celebration on completion of the holy month of Ramadaan
Ek en die kind is mense – (Afrikaans) The child and I are people
Fajr – (Arabic) early morning prayer performed by a Muslim before sunrise
falooda – (Persian) drink made by adding rose syrup to milk
fooi – (Gujerati) father's sister
gaam – (Gujerati) village
garam masala – (Gujerati) blend of ground spices used extensively in Indian cuisine
ghas – (Gujerati) China grass
ghee – (Gujerati) clarified butter
gogo – (Zulu) grandmother or elderly female person
Group Areas Act – Act no 41 of 1950 which decreed that different races must live in different areas
Gujerati – one of the languages spoken by people originating from the Gujarat area in India
Haaji – (Arabic) title given to a Muslim person who has successfully completed the Hajj to Makkah
Hadith – (Arabic) reports, statements or actions of the Prophet Muhammad (SAW)
Hajj – (Arabic) pilgrimage to the holy lands of Makkah; a religious duty that should be performed by every able-bodied Muslim at least once in his or her lifetime

halaal – (Arabic) term designating an action or object as permissible according to Islamic law
halqah– (Arabic) Quran study group
Hava Nagila – (Hebrew) Jewish traditional folk song in Hebrew
Hazrat – (Arabic) title used honour a person
Haram – (Arabic) forbidden
hidayat – (Arabic) a sense of divine guidance
hijab – (Arabic) any head, face, or body covering worn by Muslim women or men that conforms to a standard of modesty
Imam – (Arabic) person holding an Islamic leadership position; often the worship leader of a mosque and Muslim community
Insha'Allah – (Arabic) God willing
istikhara – (Arabic) prayer performed in order to receive divine guidance from Allah
izzat – (Hindi) honour
Ja, wat jy soek? – (Afrikaans, colloquial) Yes, what do you want?
jadoo – (Persian) magic
jamaat – (Arabic) group of theologians
janaaza – (Arabic) Muslim burial ceremony
Jannah – (Arabic) Paradise
Kaaba – the structure built by Prophet Ebrahim (Abraham) in Makkah, symbolising the oneness of God
kabrastaan – (Arabic) cemetery
kalya – (Gujerati) meat dish made with yogurt
Kanam / Kanamia – people originating from a region in Gujarat, India
katchoomer – (Gujerati) finely chopped salad
khaakhi shifa – sand from the holy city of Makkah
khala or khalama – (Gujerati) mother's sister
Kholvad – people originating from a region in Gujarat, India
khuri kitchree – (Gujerati) rice dish usually prepared with fish and potatoes
kurta – (Persian) loosely fitting, long shirt worn by males
laat lammetjie – (Afrikaans) a child who is born some years after his or her siblings
Lenz – shortened version of Lenasia, a small Indian town in the south of Johannesburg
ludu – board game for two to four players

Madiba – (isiXhosa) clan name of Nelson Mandela, former president of South Africa
madressah – (Arabic) institution for acquiring Islamic knowledge
MahabbaLillah – (Arabic) For the sake of Allah alone
Makkah – city in Saudi Arabia where the Kaaba is situated
mamajee – (Gujerati) mother's brother
masala – (Urdu) mixture of spices used for cooking
masjid – (Arabic) mosque/place of worship for followers of Islam
mataaf – (Arabic) area around the Kaaba on which pilgrimage rituals are performed.
Memon – people who originate from a region in North India
mendhi – (Hindi) dye used to make patterns on a girl's hand or a woman's hand; also commonly known as henna
moore – derogatory term used for Indians
Moulana – (Arabic) title given to Muslim religious leaders and graduates of religious institutions
mugh – (Gujerati) lentil
Muharram – (Arabic) the first month in the Islamic calendar
musalla – (Arabic) prayer mat
naana – (Gujerati) maternal grandfather
nafs – (Arabic) ego or soul
nanima – (Gujerati) maternal grandmother
naseeb – (Arabic) fortunate, blessed
nazar – (Arabic) look or stare to bring evil or misfortune
nikah – (Arabic) Muslim marriage contract
oomi – (Arabic) mother
ouma – (Afrikaans) grandmother
padkos – (Afrikaans) food packed for eating while travelling (literally translated as "food for the road")
panchat – (Gujerati) gossip
panjabi – (Gujerati) traditional dress worn by women
purdah – (Arabic) veil worn by Muslim women to cover their faces
puri – (Gujerati) unleavened bread
qadr – (Arabic) power
Quran – the Muslim holy book

RA – (Arabic) honorific term used for companions of the Prophet Muhammad and scholars of Islam
Rabb – (Arabic) Lord or sustainer
rakaat – (Arabic) prescribed movements and words followed by Muslims while offering prayer
Ramadaan – (Arabic) ninth month of the Muslim calendar, during which Muslims observe fasting
roti – (Gujerati) bread made from stoneground wholemeal flour
roza – (Arabic) the act of abstaining from food, drink and intercourse from sunrise until sunset (fasting)
salaah – (Arabic) practice of formal worship in Islam
samoosa – (Persian) baked or fried triangular-shaped savory
SAW – (Arabic) Peace be upon him
shambok – (Afrikaans) heavy leather whip
Sheikh – (Arabic) Islamic scholar who is awarded the title after graduation
shukr/shukran – (Arabic) thank you
sindhi – (Gujerati) sweets or gifts given out at a wedding reception
Subhanallah – (Arabic) Glorious is God
Sufi – practitioners of the inner mystical dimensions in Islam
Sunnah – (Arabic) any action which was said, done or liked by the holy prophet Muhammad (SAW)
surah – (Arabic) chapter in the holy Quran
Surtee – people originating from a region in Surat, India
Tablighi – (Arabic) Muslim religious movement aimed at spiritual reformation
tafseer – (Arabic) critical explanation or interpretation of the Quraan
tahajjud – (Arabic) voluntary prayer, also known as the night prayer, performed by followers of Islam
tajweed – (Arabic) rules governing pronunciation during recitation of the Quran
taqdeer – (Arabic) doctrine of fate or pre-destination
taqwa – (Arabic) Islamic concept of self-awareness
tarkari – (Gujerati) spicy curry
Tawakkal Allah – (Arabic) Trust in Allah
Taweez – (Arabic) written prayer from the Quran or Hadith
taweez – (Arabic) written prayer from the Quran or Hadith to be worn.

Tawheed – (Arabic) believing in the oneness of Allah
tazkiya – (Arabic) purification of the soul
ummah – (Arabic) nation or community
Umrah – pilgrimage made to the holy lands of Makkah which can take place any time of the year except during the Hajj period
vagaar – (Gujerati) fried onions used in Indian cuisine
vengra – (Gujerati) egg plant
vuvuzela – (Zulu) plastic horn that produces a loud, monotonous note and is usually blown at soccer matches in South Africa
Waar is die mense? – (Afrikaans) Where are the people?
wali – (Arabic) custodian, protector or guardian
walimah – (Arabic) the second of the two traditional parts of a Muslim wedding, generally hosted by the groom's family
Wathint'Abafazi, wathint'imbokodo! – (Zulu) Now you have touched the women, you have struck a rock!
Well of Zam Zam – the water well located within the Kaaba in Makkah
wohw – (Gujerati) daughter-in-law
yarmulke – (Hebrew) Jewish head covering worn to show respect for God
zozo – (isiZulu) a tiny house made of wood or corrugated sheeting

Notes

i "Traditional" in this context implies that the author's parents followed specific religious customs and beliefs that have existed, unchanging, for a long time.

ii Dowry amount is the mandatory amount of money paid by the groom to the bride at the time of marriage for her exclusive use.

ii Matrimonial property regimes are systems of property ownership between spouses stating how property will be managed, divided and inherited at the end of the marriage.

iv "To tie one's camel" – a proverb meaning to take responsibility for choices made.

v The Truro was the ship (from Madras) containing the first batch of 342 indentured Indian labourers to arrive in Port Natal (present Durban) on 16 November 1860.

Lightning Source UK Ltd.
Milton Keynes UK
UKHW03f1035280318
320173UK00002B/375/P

9 781920 590321